# Female-Led Relationship Guide

## How to Be a Femdom and Have the Perfect Female Domination Domestic Discipline Marriage or Relationship

**Conner Hayden**

# Table of Contents

# Introduction

"We need not just a new generation of leadership but a new gender of leadership." -William J . Clinton

You've likely heard the term 'femdom' before, but what does it mean? How can it apply to your current relationship? A femdom translates to female domination, and this doesn't necessarily have to become associated with the whips and chains depicted in pop culture or pornography. While you might be kinky as a couple, being with a femdom means that you are in a female-led relationship (FLR). You don't necessarily have to participate in anything kinky or BDSM-related if you wish to turn your relationship into an FLR. In short, the woman calls the shots. From what you do in the bedroom to what you do around the house, the woman is in charge. While femdoms have become quite the topic for fetishization, there are plenty of women who live their regular lives in FLRs with happy partners.

When you've been with your partner for a while, there is a chance that your love life has become stale. This isn't necessarily your fault because it tends to happen to couples all the time. What matters now is your willingness to put in some more effort and make the relationship exciting again. Becoming an FLR is definitely one way that you can revamp your current relationship, but both partners have to be consenting. While the concept sounds enticing, you both might be scared about what others will think or about the judgment that you will face. The great news is, what goes on behind closed doors is no one else's business. Many FLR couples only practice their ways in the privacy of their own home, but to the rest of the world, they look like a traditional couple.

Women have become very powerful in the last decade, finding new ways to become independent. Studies have shown that men who desire FLRs simply want more female authority in their lives. Again, not every aspect of an FLR has to do with sex or what goes on in the bedroom. Whether the man would like to be told what to do or bound and gagged, these are both different levels of an FLR relationship. Neither one is better than the other, and the stigma that one is perverted and one is normal needs to be erased. As long as you aren't hurting anyone or involving anyone non-consensually, then you aren't doing anything wrong in your love life.

A neuroanatomical study from the International Journal of Collaborative Research on Internal Medicine & Public Health illustrates some relevant figures on men's and women's brains. According to the review, the male brain is an average of 10-12% larger than the female brain. This is due to males having larger craniums. However, female brains actually have larger volumes in their frontal and medial paralimbic cortices (Hasan & Fauzi, 2012). This is the part of the brain that dictates decision-making. That said, most women are able to act in a femdom role when given an opportunity, even if she has never dominated before. Turning your current relationship into an FLR might be exactly what you need to boost excitement levels and give your woman her chance to shine.

As you follow these strategies, know that you are not the only couple on this path. There are hundreds of thousands of other couples who choose to live this way and enjoy every second of it. I've seen examples of many of these couples through my years as a professional relationship counselor. My specialty is assisting couples out of rough patches and dealing with intimacy issues because, as you know, all relationships are going to lead to these issues eventually. Aside from my professional life, I have personally been in several great relationships that looked right on paper but felt wrong inside. I always felt that something was missing, even though I was with great women who provided me with everything that I needed.

After seeing a relationship counselor myself, I was informed that I was seeking domination. At first, I rejected the idea but after a while I set aside the judgment and looked at the bigger picture. It was a stronger female authority that I craved. So, that began my search for a woman who could become my femdom. Through my own personal experience, I learned that this can often be a taboo subject. Many of my clients are hesitant to even mention the idea, but in the hopes of normalizing the culture, I hope that I can take this hidden desire and turn it into a normal topic of conversation.

# Chapter 1:

# FLR—What Is It?

From the brief introduction, you've gathered that an FLR is a relationship that is solely led by the female counterpart. A lot of men confuse the topic of female domination with feminism, but the two are actually very different. A feminist believes that all beings should have equal rights, often fighting for female equality because men tend to have an advantage in most areas of life. From pay rate to preferential treatment, men typically have an upper-hand in today's society. A femdom differs from a feminist because she wishes to control men. She loves to tell them what to do and how to act; her mission isn't equality, but instead, obedience.

One reason why a man might gain interest in becoming a part of an FLR might have to do with sexual fantasy. A lot of men have fantasies about their women and being told what to do. FLRs take this fantasy to a whole new level. Instead of stopping in the bedroom, the lifestyle continues as a normal and regular part of a couple's day. Some couples are more open about their FLR than others, and that comes down to personal preference. You might feel embarrassed, at first, to share this part of yourself with the rest of the world. The great thing is, you don't have to. You don't have to reveal anything about your love life unless you and your partner are both comfortable with it.

On the other hand, an FLR might start because the woman feels that she needs to play a bigger role in the relationship. Instead of sitting on the sidelines and waiting for her man to lead the way, she prefers to make the important decisions and dictate the actions. Through this authority, a different kind of chemistry can develop in the relationship, whether it is a relationship of a few months or a marriage of several years. Many couples are finding that FLRs are actually saving their relationships by renewing a sexual desire for one another through non-sexual aspects of the relationship. For example, the woman may decide where to go for dinner or how the house needs to look.

# What's the Point of Female-Led Relationships?

There isn't only one single answer to this question. Some couples find that an FLR is sexy and increases the desire for one another, while other couples find it satisfying to rebalance the power structure in their traditional relationship. Entering into an FLR, or turning your current relationship into an FLR, is a personal decision to make. Generally speaking, these relationships can be very fun and exciting because the typical roles had been reversed. The relationship experiences can also be unpredictable, ensuring that the pair does not grow bored with one another or the structure of the relationship.

## Female vs. male

Many wonder why it is the female who should dominate instead of the male. While there are relationships out there that do focus on male domination in both a traditional sense as well as a BDSM sense, female domination is not as common. It is something different and unusual for most couples. While you might have experimented in the bedroom a few times by letting your lady call the shots, have you ever lived your entire life by her instructions? While male dominance and equality, in general, are also relevant and important relationship styles, FLRs simply come down to personal preference.

A femdom does not hate her man. In fact, she cares for him deeply. That is another thing that is often misunderstood about any sort of power-play relationship. A femdom will typically put herself first, but she does care about and value her man. She is just going to have a different way of showing it. Once men experience the feeling of domination, it can often be life-changing. Men aren't typically put into situations where they feel submissive, so when they are with a femdom, a whole new side can surface. Most men find great enjoyment in being dominated, and once they give in, they find it fairly easy to submit to their femdom.

## *Differences you can see*

You might be wondering how this lifestyle will impact your relationship. It will start by rearranging all the rules you thought you knew. Instead of the man being the primary decision-maker, the woman takes over this role. As a man, you might feel more nurtured and taken care of because of this. As a woman, this role provides you with a greater purpose in the relationship. While you have decisions to make, you also have to take care of your submissive man. You can treat him how you wish to treat him, and you can make him do things for you that puts your satisfaction first. A lot of women, particularly in traditional heterosexual relationships, find that they are unsatisfied a lot. This is because men put themselves first.

Sexually speaking, men can usually get off faster than women. Once a man gets off, he is usually done with the sexual experience and needs time to rest and regroup before being able to orgasm again. Females are different because they can orgasm multiple times. In FLRs, the femdom will usually get her sexual satisfaction first before giving in to the man. This is one of the main differences that you will notice in an FLR vs. a traditional relationship. The femdom will show a sense of value over her own satisfaction and desire instead of automatically doing her 'womanly duty' to serve her man. Society has ingrained this type of message into all of us throughout the evolution of society—men are dominant, and women are obedient. Femdoms change this narrative.

## The Woman's Perspective

A lot of women are sick of being put second in life. From the way that they are treated in the professional world to the way that they must be homemakers in their personal lives. Being a femdom is a woman's chance to take back her freedom and explore new sides to herself that society has been stifling for years. A lot of women find being a femdom fun and exciting. Not all women are going to get out the whips and put on the latex, but just by having more say about what goes on in the bedroom will feel like an overall improvement in the quality of the relationship.

Happiness is experienced by a lot of women who have never been dominant before, and are now in dominant relationship roles. They are happy because they do not have to answer to anyone; they are free to make the rules and enforce them, as necessary. When a woman has this kind of control, she is less likely to blame her partner for any shortcomings that happen within the relationship. Instead, she will be able to see the bigger picture, and then she will have to decide how to proceed in order to keep the relationship vivacious.

Pornography is often one of the first introductions that women get to the femdom lifestyle. While not all pornography is a great source of education, femdom porn can actually depict a portion of the lifestyle in a way that the woman can see herself living it, too. While any femdom porn is likely going to be pretty BDSM-heavy, it will show you the dynamic held between the two individuals. Often, femdoms make their men beg or ask for things in the bedroom instead of automatically satisfying them in the ways they know how. They will also, as mentioned, place more of a priority on their own satisfaction. This might mean that the man will make the woman have several orgasms before he is even touched.

The level that you take your FLR to depends on how comfortable you and your partner are. You can't expect to go from a traditional relationship dynamic straight into a BDSM FLR. It takes experience and a transition to do this effectively. When you are changing such a big aspect of your relationship, know that it is perfectly okay to do it in steps. Start by having the woman make all of the executive decisions. From what you eat for dinner to what movies you watch, shift this control over to her. Once this becomes comfortable, you can switch up the roles in the bedroom. Hand complete control over to her. Once she has this control, she can do what she wants with it. She might not wait to satisfy you until she has been satisfied, but there might be some days where that is exactly what she desires.

As a man, it can be hard to give up this control. In society, it is programmed into men that they need to take charge and responsibility because they are strong and tough. Being in an FLR challenges this stereotype by showing men that it is okay to feel the need to be taken care of. It is okay to let a female figure take authority over his life. Letting go of control is one of the necessary components of having a successful FLR. Women find it easier to take control, but it is typically harder for the men to release their own control.

## How Will This Change the Relationship?

The obvious benefits of being in an FLR come from the enhanced sexual relationship that you will experience. Men typically find it sexy when a woman knows what she wants. If your relationship has been void of any sexual chemistry lately, then an FLR will likely take you back to what this attraction was like at the beginning of the relationship. You won't be able to keep your hands off of one another, unless she tells you to, of course. Most couples transition into an FLR for sexual reasons, but these aren't the only reasons and benefits to become a part of the lifestyle.

Intimacy aside, men deserve to be taken care of too. A man might go his whole adult life without the feeling of being nurtured or truly cared for in that way. An FLR gives him this comfort while also allowing the female counterpart of the relationship to benefit from the experience. While the female has control in the relationship, it is still often seen that both parties find great enjoyment surrounding many aspects of their FLR often in ways that they never expected. Getting over the stigma that surrounds alternative lifestyles will fully allow you the benefits that an FLR has to offer.

The dynamic will shift, and this can sometimes impact the relationship greatly or only very slightly. The degree of impact has a lot to do with your personality types and how you feel about one another. Some couples say that the dynamic truly isn't much different and that they haven't even noticed the shift. Others have reported that it is a drastic change, and it makes the relationship feel new and exciting. The fun part about engaging in an FLR for the first time is that you won't know what to expect. You won't know exactly what it will do for your dynamic until you are experiencing it for yourself.

One great thing is that you can change your mind. If the femdom lifestyle isn't right for you, then no one is going to force you to stay with it. Couples experiment all the time, and you can consider an FLR on a trial basis until you both feel comfortable with the way that things are progressing. Remember, any healthy relationship is built on consent. As long as you are both consenting to what is happening and communicating along the way, then the experience is likely impacting your relationship in a positive way. If one partner begins to feel violated or wronged, then it might not be the lifestyle for you. That's okay! You don't have to stay with it.

Another concern that couples have about their potential FLR is explaining it to their loved ones. You don't have to say a word about your personal life to anyone else if you don't want to. There are different levels to the femdom lifestyle, and if you are not comfortable with the idea of bossing your man around in public, then you can save that dynamic for when you are behind closed doors. Do not let society pressure you into thinking you are wrong or perverted for having sexual preferences. As stated, as long as you aren't hurting anyone in the process, then you are doing nothing wrong. Many couples find this secrecy to be a turn-on, anyway.

## Relevant Terms

With any alternative lifestyle, there comes a set of terminology that you should allow yourself to become familiar with. These terms might not all have relevance to you, but you should still be aware of them in case you are curious about what something means:

Vanilla Life: This refers to a lifestyle that is known as the traditional heterosexual relationship. When someone is 'vanilla,' this indicates that they prefer sex without any kinky or BDSM elements. For example, this lifestyle might include sex in the missionary position without any use of toys or props. It is not a negative term, but it is often thought of as a simple lifestyle within the FLR community. Aside from sexual preferences, the vanilla lifestyle utilizes traditional male/female roles, where the man is typically in charge of the decision-making and acts more dominant. Again, there is nothing wrong with being vanilla because it all comes down to personal preference.

Femdom: You should be familiar with this term by now—female domination. This refers to any female who enjoys dominating other individuals. This can be taken in a sexual connotation, as well as a general connotation. A femdom loves to take charge and give orders, both inside and outside of the bedroom. It is a lifestyle choice that will often lead to FLRs, and it is becoming increasingly popular in society today.

Domestic Discipline: This refers to a relationship where the head of the household is in charge of the other partner. Due to this role, the DD can make a set of rules and consequences for the partner. The punishments for breaking these rules can vary, and they are up to the DD's discretion. This type of relationship element differs from BDSM because the punishments are non-sexual.

BDSM: This is a lifestyle that stands for Bondage and Discipline, Dominance and Submission, Sadism and

Masochism. As you can see, this can tie into an FLR very well, depending on how kinky you and your partner plan on getting. BDSM is actually quite popular nowadays, and it is becoming less taboo because people are more educated on the topic than they used to be.

DD/LG: This stands for Daddy Dom and Little Girl. This relationship is quite the opposite of an FLR. In this case, the male takes on the dominant role and treats the female as his little one. He gets to decide what she wears, eats, and does on a daily basis. The LG enjoys this guidance and willingly submits to her 'Daddy.'

If these terms are new to you, do your best to learn and open your mind to them. Understand that they are all very different lifestyle choices. While they are all valid, not all of them are going to be right for you and your partner. You have the ability to experiment and decide on which lifestyle you can both identify with, and that is great! As long as you are both consenting to this experimental phase, you can try out new things until you both find the things that you enjoy the most. These terms can be overwhelming for some couples, but this usually only happens when they do not understand what the words and acronyms mean or entail. This is why education will allow for more self-discovery in your current relationship.

# FLR and BDSM

Now that you are more familiar with both terms, it is important that you understand that they don't necessarily come together automatically. Some FLRs do include a BDSM element, and this can range from light discipline to harsher pain. Your FLR does not have to include any BDSM at all if that is what you and your partner choose. Punishment is an element that tends to come naturally when there is a relationship in which one partner is 100% dominant. This punishment does not have to be physical, though. It can be subtle, yet still remain effective.

If you'd like to experiment with punishments, yet you do not want to inflict any type of pain on your partner, you can try to provide them with chores or duties to fulfill. These tasks can be anything from doing housework to running errands. If the female wants something, she can make the male go out and get it for her as a punishment for being disobedient. These are just some examples, but you should know that there are many degrees and variations of involvement in an FLR, much like any other lifestyle.

For something that is a little bit more exciting and passionate, you can create sexual punishments for your partner. These can involve anything from them having to pleasure you until you tell them to stop, to any number of humiliations at their expense. Since the female is in charge, her preferences are going to shape the form of sexual punishments that she decides on. Another form of punishment can be withholding sexual contact. This is one that typically drives the male crazy, and makes him work hard to please the female.

If you decide to get into BDSM, make sure that you do it safely. There is a proper way to choke your partner and whip your partner sexually without inflicting extremely serious damage. It is a smart idea to read up on the topic and get truly familiar with it before you attempt to incorporate it into your life. From different bondage techniques to sadistic punishments, BDSM can be a very exciting change for a couple, especially when coming from a vanilla lifestyle.

A lot of couples are very unsure about inflicting harm on one another, but the bondage aspect can sound intriguing. This involves tying one partner up and then, potentially, performing sexual actions on them. Sometimes, the action of tying your partner up is the intimate action on its own. Of course, in an FLR, the female would be in charge of the rope. She would be able to tie her partner up as necessary, and from there, she could do whatever she wanted to him.

Again, no BDSM relationship is going to look the same. There are so many elements involved that you can truly customize it to work with your current FLR. Whether you want to go all-out or only try one or two new things, that decision is going to be up to you. This kind of exploration is great and healthy for a relationship. If it is very different than what you are used to as a couple, it is an automatic way to make the relationship feel more exciting. A lot of couples can probably vouch for BDSM as a reason for their relationship's revitalization.

# FLR and Feminism

Another comparative analysis, this section takes a look at why an FLR and feminism are not the same things. While the female in an FLR can definitely hold feminist values outside of her love life, the mindset is incredibly different when she is in control of her partner. Being in an FLR means that the female is in charge, no matter what. She gets to be dominant, and this goes without any question. The female in an FLR believes that it is her right to make these decisions, and potentially manipulate her partner to her liking. She gets everything she wants when she wants it.

Unfortunately, many people still do not understand that the core of feminism is equality for *all*. Feminists do not believe that females are superior, but rather, due to female-exclusive adversities that have been continually faced throughout society, females statistically have to work harder to achieve what males can by default. This fight for equality focuses on setting the standards straight and creating a more balanced society where women are treated equally.

Taking a look at the two, you can already see how an FLR and feminism are radically different. A lot of people who are uneducated on both topics often confuse feminism with man-hating. The same can also be said for FLR relationships. Ironically, neither one involves the hatred of men. In fact, it is safe to say that both can include a great love for men. This feeling is just expressed very differently, respectively. Make sure that you understand the differences between the two terms. There is currently a lot of misinformation being spread about both, so when you have this knowledge handy, you can help others understand.

There is no doubt that an FLR and feminism do have some striking similarities. For one, both involve females taking control. Though this happens in very different ways with different intended outcomes, you can still see the pattern of female-led action that is happening within each one. A lot of traditional vanilla men are angered by the idea of both because they feel that both concepts encroach on their masculinity. This is a struggle that many FLR females and feminists both have to deal with. In reality, none of these females have the virtue of destroying masculinity. They each simply have the desire to make a change and get what they want.

This is why the topic of an FLR can often seem taboo because it can be widely misunderstood. While you can do your best to correct people and explain the differences between your relationship and feminism, there will always be some that just do not understand. In this case, you need to let bygones be bygones. People with traditional values ingrained into their social morals have a hard time letting go of what they have known their whole lives. This is understandable if you think about it as a whole. If your relationship isn't hurting anyone or impacting anyone outside of yourself and your partner, then you are doing nothing wrong and do not require anyone an explanation.

## A Natural Evolution?

Many people believe that a female-led relationship is a natural evolution. With past societies being ruled by men with voting-rights held only by men, it seems that it was only a matter of time before the female revolution began. Though females now have a lot more rights in today's modern society, there is still a past cultural pressure that is placed on females to act and look a certain way. This is a unique pressure that is not necessarily placed as heavily on males. Most of the time, men do not even notice this, and it is due to their privilege.

Men can make mistakes and learn from them; women are blamed for the mistakes of men. Rape culture is a very prevalent issue today. When a woman gets raped by a man, some of the first questions include what she was wearing and where she was. Society's first instinct is to find something incriminating about the woman in order to place the blame on her. It is a rarity that people turn their focus on the man, feeling outraged by his behavior and desire to rape a woman in the first place. This is why women feel that it is hard to speak up about these issues—often, they aren't believed.

When it comes to the professional world, men are seen as the dominant gender. If you ask any woman you know, she can likely express that she has felt sexism, even sexual harassment, in her workplace. Men are given promotions over women all the time, and they are even paid more on a regular basis. In order to make what a man makes, a woman typically has to work harder. This can naturally contribute to a lot of frustration and anger when it comes to women's rights and equality. This is how society is shaping women today, and a lot of people believe that this is why many couples' relationships are naturally evolving into FLRs.

While there are many other factors involved when deciding on embarking upon an FLR (such as the simple enjoyment of the dynamic), women tend to feel as though this lifestyle is an outlet for all of the frustration that they have been holding in for years. In a society that typically works against them, stripping them of rights and making a mockery out of their suffering, they finally get to regain control. In today's society, more women are taking charge in more ways. Whether it is in an FLR or in the workplace, women are helping one another become braver and more vocal about relevant issues.

Though there might not be any science to it, simply the beginning of a new kind of era, females have been on the rise in the last decade. They have realized that they are done putting up with things that they should not have to put up with, and they want men to realize that their experiences of the same situations can be incredibly different. When everyone is able to see eye-to-eye, this is when true equality can be achieved. Sometimes, the focus needs to be on justice rather than giving everybody the same opportunities. Even with the exact same resources, if women are being treated as less, then there is still injustice happening. While nothing is promised to change overnight, the idea of having an FLR can help to get women one step closer to the roles they truly desire. Women can do anything they want to do, and this has been proven over and over again.

# Chapter 2:

# Levels and Roles

It has been mentioned a few times throughout this text, but it is essential to realize that there are different levels when it comes to an FLR lifestyle. There are also designated roles that the couple will have to assign as this relationship develops. There is much more to an FLR than simply deciding one day that the woman is going to boss the man around. This chapter takes an in-depth look at just how many levels and roles there can be within this alternative relationship style. By learning about each one, you will have more insight as to what sounds best for your own personal relationship.

Know that, just like any other relationship, roles can change at any time. If you find that something isn't working in your FLR, then your female counterpart has the ability to make adjustments. The great thing about experimenting with your relationship dynamic is that it does not have to be set in stone. You both might find something that you truly enjoy at first, but then it could evolve into something that you don't care for anymore. Being able to switch this dynamic and assign new roles is exciting, and it shows that there is truly no reason for your relationship to become boring again.

## The Submissive Male and Dominant Female

In a typical FLR, a day in the life can look a little something like this:

- The couple wakes up, and the man makes breakfast (of the woman's choosing, of course).

- They part ways as they go to work.

- After work, the male will run any necessary errands, such as going to the grocery store.

- Once at home, the female does as she pleases; the male does housework and cooks dinner.

- If the couple decides to go out to eat, the male will pay (unless the female is in the mood to pay).

- Anything done for the purpose of relaxation or entertainment is selected by the female. This can sometimes involve the male, yet sometimes it involves alone time.

- In the bedroom, if the couple decides to have sex, this can go several different ways. Depending on the female's mood, she might want to be pleasured, and then they will go to bed.

- Alternatively, she might want to be pleasured and she might keep the male on edge.

- Another possibility is when the female makes the male work toward his reward (sexual pleasure). Depending on the level of BDSM involved, the steps can vary.

- In regards to general life decisions, the female makes them on behalf of a couple.

- If they get invited out by another couple or individual, the female decides if they are going or not.

- If the male wants plans on his own to see friends or have alone time, he must ask the female for permission.

- No matter what, the male is always trying to make his female happy.

This is a loose reference to follow for the standard FLR. While all relationships are unique due to the individuals involved, you can get an idea for the kind of dynamic that can be expected, whether you are the submissive male or the dominant female. Of course, if anything about this dynamic sounds wrong to you, then it likely isn't going to work for your relationship. In an FLR, the man is *eager* to please his woman. This means that he wants her to be happy, in general, as well as sexually satisfied at all times. He does not have a problem with being put on the back burner when it comes to giving her what she wants.

The female is in a position of great power. She gets to oversee the entire relationship as though it is her own personal project. If she feels that the man has done a great job of obeying her, she might reward him with small instances of independence or more sexual pleasure. However, if she feels that he has not been an obedient sub (submissive), then the punishment can begin. As discussed, the punishment is going to vary per couple. It can be physical, emotional, both, or neither. The female might decide that the male can't participate in a hobby he likes for a week as a punishment. Alternatively, the female might decide that a proper punishment is not allowing the male to get off sexually for a week.

The dynamic is so interesting because the passion does not come from a power struggle. There is no question that the female has the power, and the male wouldn't dare to try and take it from her. They each enjoy their respective positions in the relationship. Depending on how comfortable the couple is with their lifestyle, they might enjoy displaying small parts of it while they are around friends and family. A subtle way to prove that the woman is in control while in public would be deciding what the male is going to eat. A lot of people might not catch on to this nuance, but both parties would know exactly what it means and where they stand. If the man were to disobey and eat something different, there would surely be consequences to face once the couple got home.

While it sounds like one big game, the best way to make an FLR work is to take it very seriously. Once you are given a role, stay in the role. The only time you should stray is if you feel that the lifestyle truly isn't working for your relationship. It does take time to find out, though. Give it at least a month, and see how the dynamic shifts as you both become more comfortable with your respective roles. It definitely isn't going to work if one partner is taking it seriously while the other is laughing on the sidelines. Both parties must be consensual and committed.

As you can see, an FLR does not necessarily revolve around a couple's sexual habits. While sex can be an aspect of the relationship, you can still have a valid FLR without even having sex at all. The main point is that the woman is always going to be in a greater position of power than the man, and he is going to enjoy taking on a submissive role. If you need to start by shifting these roles in your daily life, you can do this before you make the sexual shift. This transition can sometimes make it easier to remember where you stand in the relationship and how you are supposed to behave now.

# Female Role Variations

Did you know that the dominant female can play specific roles in the relationship? When you are in an FLR, you are going to realize that your female partner is going to find her favorite way of being in control. And yes, there is more than one way. The following are some roles to become familiar with that pertain to being a femdom and what they mean:

Dominatrix: A dominatrix usually refers to a woman who does enjoy some BDSM play. The level of this play can still vary, but a woman like this enjoys punishing her man and creating a reward system. She is going to be very observant of his behaviors, judging if he is worthy. She might even make her man worship her on occasion. If physical domination isn't occurring, then you can guarantee that there will be an element of mental domination. She might degrade the man, but he will know that he deserves it.

Cuckoldress: This is a woman who regularly sleeps with other people because it brings the man pleasure. The man will often encourage the woman to go out and be with others, and ultimately, she will if she feels like it. This can be one aspect of the cuckoldress. The other aspect deals with humiliation and degradation. Often, a cuckoldress will regularly humiliate her partner and degrade him. She might even make him do demeaning activities as she watches in enjoyment. This is an intense role to be played, and the male does not always receive enjoyment from each aspect of it.

Hot Wife: The female might take on the hot wife persona, meaning she enjoys taking on the role of being the perfect homemaker and great partner. Regarding sexual relationships, she is encouraged by her male partner to sleep with other people. He will feel proud that this is his sexy partner, and he might even watch her engage in sexual activity with others. In this sort of dynamic, the male does get enjoyment out of what is going on. He will often suggest that his woman finds other people to sleep with as a way to fulfill both of their fantasies.

All of these roles can vary to a certain degree. They must be applicable to the woman's personality type. If the woman in the relationship is typical private or introverted, you likely wouldn't expect her to become a dominatrix who takes action in public on her sub. On the other hand, if the woman tends to be more open and extroverted, she might be very public about her hot wife lifestyle. It is important to remember that your individual personalities are going to change the dynamics above. While you might not be able to directly relate with any of these roles yet, you can try them out for yourself and see how they make you feel.

With any kind of FLR, there comes a lot of trial and error. You both have to realize that your female might have to take on several different roles until she finds the one that she likes best, and that is okay. As a male, it is his job to be flexible and willing to explore each of these changes with her until she decides what works best. The level of public domination that is done can also vary greatly. As mentioned, you might not want to be public with your lifestyle at all in the beginning because it is still so new to both of you. The good news is—you don't have to! There is no deadline for revealing this new aspect of your relationship with anyone.

A lot of couples are incredibly kinky behind closed doors, and then they use subtleties while they are in public. This allows them to stay in their roles while also being very discreet. It can become more fun when only you two know what is really going on. For example, the woman might decide that the couple is going to eat dinner at a restaurant. For an added element of fun and control, she might make the man wear a ball clamp the entire time, only to take it off once they get back home. This is a way that the female is still establishing that she has total control of her partner, but onlookers likely would never be able to tell exactly what is going on. In fact, you might know some FLR couples yourself, and you likely don't even realize it. With its rise in popularity, you never know how many other couples have already decided to take on this alternative lifestyle.

## Male Role Variations

The male has a very simple role in an FLR, and that is to be submissive. This can greatly vary depending on what type of female partner he has. Whether he is with a hardcore dominatrix or a woman who is simply testing out the boundaries of being in control, the male needs to adjust to the woman's liking. It can start out slow at first, but it will often pick up speed the more that the woman starts enjoying her power. As a submissive male, there isn't too much variation. The most important thing is that you act obediently at all times. If your female counterpart has a request, you better do your best to fulfill it. If punishment is involved, you can expect to be punished a lot if you aren't quite making ends meet.

Some men can be submissive while holding on to their original personality types. This means that they enjoy being themselves, yet they take orders from their female partner. Other men, the ones who prefer to be degraded, might be referred to as 'sissies.' A sissy loves to be degraded and humiliated by his partner. This embarrassment might actually cause him to feel some sexual pleasure. Of course, in order to act like a sissy, it is important that the man is with a woman who can fill the correct role as well. If he is with a woman who does not enjoy degrading men, then the dynamic won't work.

There are a handful of men who might test their females from time to time, experimenting with what happens if they disobey her requests. These men will likely get punished frequently. If the woman catches on to this behavior, she might not punish the man in order to spite him since she realizes that he is enjoying the punishment. Instead, she might switch it up and make him do something that she knows he will not get any pleasure from. Of course, these situations are all subjective because each individual is going to have their own preferences.

As a man, there really isn't much work to be done in determining what type of submissive you are going to be. This is for the female to decide. The only thing that needs to be kept in mind is the fact that your female partner is going to tell you what should be done. If you need to act a different way, follow a new set of rules, or even dress a certain way, your femdom is going to let you know this. The man's experience in an FLR is one that comes with little responsibility until he is given a concrete role. Because he will no longer be in charge of anything around the house or the couple's social life, he must focus on his obedience more than anything.

If the female feels as though he needs to be doing more, she will let him know. As a submissive male, it is best just to let go of any and all control from the very beginning. Try to get rid of your instinct to take control and be helpful. What might appear helpful to you might be annoying to your femdom. She is going to request your help when she needs it, and you need to be waiting there until she is ready to do so. In the meantime, it is your job to simply be mindful of her needs and her preferences. Don't take any deliberate action unless you are instructed to do so. Otherwise, you might end up angering your female partner.

Femdoms love it when their men are willing to do anything at any time. This means that you have to let go of certain standards and expectations. As a male, you should not expect to be sexually pleasured any time you feel the need. This is now totally up to your female counterpart. If she decides that you deserve the pleasure, or if she feels like giving, then you will be pleased. Asking for sex or sexual acts from your femdom might result in punishment. It is always best to wait for her command, sexually. If you ask for too much, then you might end up with nothing at all.

A great sub should be very eager to please his dom. Since her pleasure is your priority, show her how much you enjoy servicing her sexually. Don't rush through it in order to get your own satisfaction quicker. She will definitely take notice of this and likely punish you or prevent you from getting off. Listen to her instructions closely, and you will both have an amazing time in bed. When a woman is given so much power, she will often transform before your eyes. Your partner, who was once a participant in your sex life, is now going to be the one who is in charge of the entire thing. This is a very exciting role to take on, and you can expect the sex to get kinkier than its ever been before.

# Dominant and Submissive Relationship Types

You can maintain a dom/sub type of relationship in more than one way. Not all FLR couples implement all of the elements of a typical dom/sub relationship into their dynamic as a couple. The most obvious way that it can be done is sexual. In the bedroom, you have probably experimented with a dom/sub type of role-play before. Whether it was the male or the female in charge, it is common for traditional couples to experiment with this at one point or another in their relationship. This tends to be the most natural way to incorporate the dom/sub dynamic into a once-traditional relationship. Couples tend to be more experimentally open in the bedroom when it comes to the kind of sex they are having.

Sex can look different in any relationship, but there is a certain dynamic that is typically present in a dom/sub relationship. The most basic concept about a dom/sub sexual relationship is that the dom tells the sub what to do. Depending on the dom's mood, this can vary. In an FLR, your femdom is going to be bossing you around. You might have to please her for hours on end, or you might have to let her do anything she wants to you. This type of dynamic is exciting and intriguing for most couples because traditional roles are disregarded. The female gets to decide what happens, and if anything sexual happens. She takes the lead, and the sub is supposed to willingly follow. If punishments are implemented, they will happen due to a sub not being obedient enough.

Another way that dom/sub couples like to push sexual boundaries is by experimenting with public play. This can mean that the sub has to wear a sex toy out of the house and be teased the entire day before coming home to his femdom. Other times, the dom might like to discreetly tease the sub when no one else is looking. This kind of foreplay can become very intense, making for some exciting sex once the couple is finally behind closed doors. It can definitely be a way for any couple to renew their passion fairly easily.

Around the house, the femdom might have a list of chores for her sub to complete. These chores might be typical household duties that a woman would normally take care of, maybe errands. The sub is supposed to have a great attitude regarding their responsibilities and will take care of them without any issues. If the femdom feels that the sub isn't doing his job properly, she might punish him or take away some of his privileges. Again, keep in mind that not all dom/sub couples utilize punishments, but the majority of them seem to find it an appropriate way to keep the sub in line.

There are always levels to every aspect of a dom/sub relationship. If you want to utilize punishments, yet you do not know where to begin, start small. Withholding sexual pleasure is a great punishment, and it does not involve any BDSM. It is simply a tactic that can be used to drive your partner crazy. Not being able to finish until the femdom has orgasmed as much as she pleases is also a great punishment to utilize. Femdoms tend to love begging—you can make your partner beg for what they want if they disobey you. Imaginably, there are thousands of ways you can punish your partner without physically hurting them.

If you decide to get into BDSM as a beginner couple, make sure that you are doing it safely. There are ways to physically harm your partner for sexual pleasure that does not involve hurting them permanently. From whipping to choking, there are many painful and pleasurable acts that the femdom can test on her sub. When you are first starting out with BDSM, you do not have to aim to be hardcore or push any boundaries that you are uncomfortable with. Go with what the femdom feels is right. Only together as a couple will you be able to discover your own personal boundaries.

Being in a dom/sub relationship is much more than just being with a bossy female. It is a way of life, and it can be implemented into every area of your life that you wish to incorporate it with. In the beginning, you are likely going to be more discreet. But after some time, your femdom might be openly ordering you around, and you will realize that you love it when other people know that she is in charge of you. Dom/sub relationships are much like traditional relationships in the sense that they fulfill the same needs to each person involved. You should feel a sense of love, loyalty, and intrigue in your dom/sub relationship.

# The Four Levels of Dominance

## *Level one*

Conditional compliance means that there is a specific power level, but it is limited. The dom can take over total control of a situation for a brief period of time, or for only certain sexual situations. The activities that occur under level one dominance are typically discussed ahead of time, giving the sub some input as to what occurs. This level is excellent for beginners who have never experienced any type of FLR or BDSM relationship before. It can become a gateway that leads to higher levels of dominance in the future.

Even if you start with a dominant sexual activity once per week, this is a perfectly valid way to enter an FLR relationship. You need to do what feels right and what allows both parties to feel comfortable. If you rush into things, they might become too overwhelming for either one or both of the individuals involved in the relationship. This is basically a way for you to have a trial and error period with your partner to decide if this is a lifestyle that will work for you. Enjoy it, and have fun with it!

## *Level two*

This level is known as the restricted and ongoing acquiescence phase. An example of this can be regular BDSM play, minus any serious emotional attachment or seriousness. This is usually what level one transforms into once both parties have become more comfortable with the shift in power and control. Level two can last for longer periods of time, perhaps weeks or months. There is still a certain sense of impermanence, though, because the sub still has a chance to leave his role after certain periods of time. However, he will often return to the submissive role before too long.

Since level two is carried out more frequently or lasts for longer periods of time, the couple can maintain a deeper dom/sub relationship than before. When something becomes habitual, it is easier to accept is as a part of your daily lifestyle and routine. The femdom gains more power than she had before, and the sub is transported even deeper into a state of submission. Level two can be your resting dominance level, or it can continue to prepare you for even higher levels of dominance in the future.

## *Level three*

This level is marked by provisional submission. The sub continues to give up even more control to the femdom. This can perhaps be noted by the sub giving up his rights to make decisions both inside and outside of the bedroom. As he eases into his role of submission, the femdom is given more control of the overall relationship dynamic. This marks an even greater expansion of the lifestyle that is typical to an FLR couple. Both parties are likely to get very comfortable with being on this level.

If BDSM is practiced, it is likely that sexual activity has become kinkier than ever. Both parties have likely reached a certain threshold of pleasure and pain that are new to them. If you are committed to an FLR relationship, at this point, you might decide to stay on this level of dominance. A lot of couples are very happy with this level of control, and the femdom is typically pleased by the sub's willingness and obedience. Because there are no time constraints, it is perfectly valid to stop at level three.

## *Level four*

This level, if reached, involves a serious emotional commitment. Explained as the covenant of dominance where both parties work symbiotically to achieve pleasure and satisfaction in every aspect of life. FLR couples who are comfortable with displaying their relationship publicly are usually on this level of dominance. It is a level that symbolizes not only sexual pleasure but great emotional pleasure as well. The femdom should feel extremely powerful in a non-conditional way. The sub should feel grateful to be controlled and guided by his femdom.

Not an act of role-playing, this level is a serious lifestyle change that will impact every aspect of how the couple operates. From trips to the grocery store to their most intimate moments in bed, level four dominance is present. The femdom is in complete control of every situation, and hardcore BSDM is likely to be practiced on a regular basis. Punishments should be set out and expectations clear. If the femdom suddenly decides that she wants to change something about the relationship, the sub has no say in whether or not it happens. He will act obediently, supporting all decisions made.

# Chapter 3:

# Rules and Conditions

In any FLR relationship, it is important to have a clear set of rules and conditions to follow at all times. This gives the femdom a chance to fully assert her power while giving the submissive male a guideline for how he is expected to act. When both individuals are fully aware of what the expectations are, this gives them the chance to focus on being better lovers and partners. It can also eliminate any confusion that is typically felt when entering an alternative lifestyle type of relationship.

You will learn how to flawlessly implement this lifestyle into your current one, easily transitioning using certain methods and techniques. By doing this in steps, both parties can feel safe and have a mutual sense of positivity regarding the relationship as a whole. Even though the female is in charge, it's likely going to still be important to her that her male partner feels safe and trusts these changes. There should be a sense of respect coming from both sides of the relationship. Otherwise, an FLR will not work out successfully.

## How to Overcome Fear/Guilt

As you further explore your boundaries as a couple, you both might feel a sense of fear or guilt over your lifestyle choice. This section covers ways to overcome the feelings and explains where they stem from. In a traditional relationship, there is usually no fear or guilt present because it abides by society's view of what is considered 'normal.' One of the very first things you both should do is get used to the idea that there is no defined view of what is normal and what is abnormal in an FLR. You both get to decide these parameters for yourself.

It is only when you can become comfortable in your own roles and the relationship that you can gain the confidence to get rid of society's view of what is considered normal. You can do so by discussing the relationship with your partner and expressing where you both would like it to go. If you have some goals that you'd like to accomplish, talk about them openly with your partner. The femdom will likely be very vocal during this conversation, expressing all of the ways she would like to dominate and control her male submissive. While the man might have some input, as well, both partners will realize that the female is ultimately going to make the final decisions.

Each individual is likely going to have unique fears or a unique sense of guilt regarding the relationship. As a female, there might be a worry that she is being too hard on her partner. Taking on a dominant role as a once-submissive individual can often feel wrong in some ways. There is definitely a lot of confidence needed in order to overcome these feelings. If you are the female counterpart in the relationship, you need to do your best to empower yourself at all times. Know that you are a strong woman who is capable of anything, and anything that you want, you deserve to have.

You will not only see improvement in your relationship when you are a more confident woman, but you will also notice differences in other aspects of your life. As a professional individual, you might see that you feel better able to work your job and get what you want out of your career. As a friend, you will be able to make better decisions as to who is serving your life in a positive way and who is dragging you down. There are so many great reasons to step aside from your fears if you are able to. Use them as motivation to reassure yourself that you are on the right path in your life.

As the male counterpart, your guilt and fears might display themselves in an entirely different way. Since society has a very clear image of what a 'real' man should look like and act like, you are likely feeling these pressures as you enter your FLR. To most people, men are seen as decision-makers. They are supposed to be tough as nails and able to guide their partner through anything that they encounter together as a couple. Remember, when you are in an FLR, you are willingly relinquishing this control. By doing this, you are receiving enjoyment and even pleasure. This is a very personal decision, and you cannot expect the outside world to understand that right away.

It is perfectly valid to keep your relationship to yourself. You do not owe anyone the details of what goes on in your FLR. If you are happy with what is happening, then you don't have to worry about what anyone else thinks about your decision. Even if you decide never to tell anyone about your alternative lifestyle, that doesn't invalidate it in the slightest. Whether you tell your loved ones, everyone you know, or nobody at all, your relationship is still going to exist as a separate and personal entity.

Fear that stems from certain activities in your relationship need to be addressed. If you are ever truly uncomfortable with something that your femdom has implemented in the relationship, then you should have a serious conversation about it. An FLR is supposed to test your limits, but it shouldn't cause you to feel any permanent distress. Of course, in doing so, you might feel guilty for disobeying your femdom's original wishes. At the end of the day, you both know each other best.

By being honest with one another in terms of what you can and cannot put up with in a relationship, you should both be able to come to a reasonable agreement about how things are going to work.

Remember, these feelings are all common. Both the femdom and the submissive male might go through phases of feeling fearful or guilty. If you can remember that what you are doing isn't wrong, then you should have no problem getting through each rough patch that you experience. If it ever becomes too much to handle, talk about it with your partner before it gets out of hand. They might be feeling the exact same way, and it is best to be open and discuss these things instead of simply waiting for them to pass on their own. Any healthy relationship requires a large amount of open communication.

Even though your relationship style is alternative, it still needs to be healthy. If it is taking a lot out of you to be in the relationship, then something likely needs to change. No matter what your role is, you should still feel happy to be with your partner in any situation or lifestyle that you decide on. A relationship that causes resentment to build up is one that is bordering on toxic. Make sure that you know the difference between a normal amount of fear/guilt because something is new and an increasing level of toxicity. As long as you are open with one another from the very beginning, there should be no reason that your relationship ever gets to a point that is so low. No matter how long you have been together, check-in with each other every so often.

# Inside the Bedroom vs. Outside the Bedroom

It goes without saying that all couples are going to be way more intimate and open in their relationships inside of the bedroom versus outside of the bedroom. Keep this in mind regarding your FLR. While the femdom might feel extremely comfortable in her role during sexual situations, she might not want to reveal this part of herself to the outside world yet (or ever). She might not even care to boss her sub around while in the house, in general. This is a common situation that is faced by a lot of couples who enter into an FLR.

The easiest step to take when transitioning the relationship's dynamic is to begin in the bedroom. This is where you should feel the most comfortable and open with your partner. Exploring sexual dominance is a very freeing feeling. The femdom has a chance to be her true self without any fear of judgment, and the submissive male can get used to taking orders from his partner. There are a few ways that you can do this if you plan to start your FLR in the bedroom before expanding it to the rest of your relationship.

Allow the femdom to tell the submissive male partner what she desires in the bedroom. Though this can change depending on her mood and the overall mood between the two individuals, she needs to speak up about what she desires. Communication is important, so both people know what is going to happen in the bedroom from now on. While the relationship might have been more sexually balanced in the past, it is important to let go of all comparisons to what you used to do together.

Some femdoms are satisfied with simply giving orders. No matter if she is telling her partner what position she wants to be in or what sexual activity she would like him to perform, she is gaining her power by dictating how the sexual encounters are now going to take place. As you become more comfortable with this FLR lifestyle, the way that the femdom dominates in the bedroom can evolve.

After your femdom is comfortable giving orders, you can try withholding. This means that the femdom gets her pleasure before the male gets any pleasure. It is up to her discretion when her partner gets to receive pleasure. The femdom might require several hours of her own pleasure before she pays any attention to the needs of her partner. It should be something enjoyable for the male sub because he will be very happy to please his femdom.

There is also the idea of edging. The femdom might give her partner sexual pleasure, but not allow him to finish. Keeping him on the edge of this feeling makes for some intense sex, and the pleasure is definitely electrifying when the man is finally allowed to finish. Because the femdom has all of the control, she gets to decide how long the man must edge for. She might even make him beg her to allow him to finish, but he is going to need her permission first.

When maximum comfort has been reached, sex can become very unpredictable for the male counterpart in the relationship. Depending on the femdom's mood, there might be a mixture of edging and withholding. Alternatively, she might solely want to please the man until she feels that she has given him as much as she wants to give him. Sex should never be planned or scheduled, but there do need to be some rules laid out so that both parties know what is to be expected. As long as the sub male obeys, then the femdom should be happy.

Some couples fully participate in the FLR lifestyle, yet they do not apply this practice outside of the bedroom. In normal daily life, nothing else might change the traditional relationship dynamic, and this is okay. An FLR does not have to follow a checklist in order to be considered an FLR. If you both as a couple agree that you'd only like to apply these rules in the bedroom, then this is entirely up to you. Once you become more comfortable with the lifestyle, there might be room for it to evolve. Make sure that you are both enjoying what you are doing, and check-in with each other often. You might decide that you would like to incorporate more dominance and submission in other aspects of your life after you become more comfortable with the sexual aspect of a dom/sub relationship.

It makes sense as to why you might think that you do not know any other FLR couples in your life. A lot of them do decide to keep things private, even strictly sexual. This is especially common for those who are beginners in the lifestyle. The only thing that you must keep in mind is that you are both happy with the way that the relationship dynamic is evolving. If you need more of something or less of something, communicate this with one another. A dom/sub relationship can turn abusive very quickly, unfortunately. This is why speaking up is imperative.

On the other hand, there are some traditional couples who enter into an FLR by doing the exact opposite—they start outside of the bedroom first. The femdom might order the male sub to do housework and perform all of the chores that would normally be considered her responsibility. Once they get used to this and realize that they are both enjoying it, then they might decide to try to switch to this dynamic in the bedroom.

A lot of men in traditional relationships do have trouble letting go of their control in the bedroom. In society, it is known that the heterosexual male needs to please his woman. He needs to take control and lead his woman into the exact kind of sexual activity that he desires. By letting go of this control, he must also be willing to let go of the pressures that society places on couples daily. Remember, if you are enjoying something and not hurting anyone in the process, then you are not doing anything wrong.

# Important Traits

## *Trust*

In any relationship, there needs to be trust present. This is especially true when entering an FLR. The male has to trust that his femdom knows exactly what needs to happen in order to have a successful and fulfilling relationship that lasts. The female needs to trust that her submissive male is going to take her seriously and obey her orders when they are given. There is also the important issue of privacy. It isn't fair when one partner is telling everyone they know about their new relationship while the other partner prefers to keep it a secret permanently. These are the things that trust will revolve around in an FLR. Without trust, the relationship isn't going to work. There will be a power struggle, and that should definitely not be present in an FLR. There should be no doubt about it that the female is in charge. If he isn't respecting her rules and guidelines, then there is no trust present between the two of them.

## *Vulnerability*

This trait mainly applies to the male sub—being able to be vulnerable is an essential factor in being a part of an FLR. The male needs to not only ignore societal pressures to hide his vulnerability, but he must be honest with himself in order to achieve it. It isn't really anything that the femdom can assist with; the male has to feel secure enough in himself and in the relationship in order to fully become vulnerable. For help with this, the male sub should begin speaking about his feelings more. Being open with his femdom is going to help him be more vulnerable. While she might not give in to all of his needs, having a listening ear is still going to help. Start by telling your femdom about your day every single day. Don't only recount the events that happened to you, but also let her know how they made you feel. The more you practice this, the easier the vulnerability will become.

## Communication

Without being stated, you should know how important communication is for any relationship. With an FLR couple, certain aspects of the relationship must be discussed before they are acted upon. It is always a good idea to get your boundaries and no-gos out of the way from the very beginning. Tell your partner what is off-limits, and come up with a safe word in case the sexual play becomes too much for you to handle. Communicating about these things *before* you enter into a full-blown FLR is going to make the relationship much more enjoyable than finding out about these boundaries along the way. Failure to communicate can cause unnecessary tension between the couple, and it might even lead to lasting resentment. Talk about other aspects of your relations that are going to occur outside of the bedroom, as well. Discuss how you'd like to act in front of other people, your family, and your loved ones. You will be able to gauge one another's comfort level when you communicate regularly and in a healthy manner.

## Humiliation

Humiliation can become a big aspect of an FLR. Some femdoms love to humiliate their men. Whether this happens privately or in public, the sub needs to be prepared to be humiliated if the femdom enjoys this type of play. Boundaries can be set when it comes to the type of humiliation that is experienced. Some femdoms will simply make their subs feel slightly uncomfortable, while others will enjoy the experience of treating them like children and making them soil themselves while wearing diapers. There are different levels and extremes for every single type of FLR humiliation play. Financial humiliation is also an option. Financial humiliation is when the femdom makes it apparent that she is paying for things and that the male has no choice but to let her. A lot of couples enjoy doing this in public, especially at restaurants, when the male is typically expected to pay in traditional heterosexual relationships. If any humiliation play is desired, you will have to decide on what you'd like to do as a couple.

## Punishment and discipline

You've experienced a little bit of what punishment and discipline can look like by reading prior sections of this guide. The choice you will have to make now is to what degree you plan to take this punishment. The femdom might have no interest in punishing her sub, or she might have a very big interest in punishment. It is a very personal decision to make. Again, this conversation needs to be taken with boundaries into account. If the male sub has expressed that he does not want to receive any punishment that involves torture or beatings, then the femdom should be able to find other ways to discipline while still respecting what he has consented to. Talking about these things ahead of time will save the femdom from feeling that she has lost her power or control. She is not going to want to feel this way when an FLR has already been developed.

## Comfort

Believe it or not, comfort is actually a huge aspect of an FLR. Most of the time, the femdom is going to take her sub's comfort into consideration. When she is not in the mood to tease or discipline, then she might treat her sub in a very adoring manner. She will likely care a great deal about his comfort. On the other hand, the sub should always take his femdom's comfort into consideration. If she is unhappy, then he needs to be looking into ways that he can improve her mood and the situation that is causing her distress. These relationships do involve some give and take, but both individuals should be aware of this before entering into an FLR. Everyone wants to be comfortable with their partners and who they are when they are with their partners. It is still important to focus on individual comfort, even when involved in a power dynamic that is entirely one-sided. Comfort is the gateway to happiness, and this should be a goal for couples who participate in all kinds of different lifestyle choices.

## Written Rules

The easiest way to keep the rules of your relationship clear is by writing them down. Once a conversation has been had regarding boundaries, safe words, and more, the femdom should create a written set of rules that the male sub can refer to. When the rules are written down, the femdom has another tool to help enforce her power. At the same time, the male has an easy-to-follow list of how he is expected to behave. Rules are beneficial for both individuals in the FLR.

Post the rules in your bedroom where only the two of you can see them. As the femdom, it can be a fun element of play to have your male sub memorize or recite these rules often. Hearing him say them out loud will provide you with even more power and control. It can also prove to be a turn on for both of you. If the femdom feels that it is necessary, she can have her sub carry the rules with him at all times. This way, even if he is at work and away from his femdom, he can be reminded of how he needs to act.

Kinky couples might enjoy adding very particular sexual rules to the list. The femdom can change these rules at her discretion, and the male must follow them, no matter what. If a rule is broken, there can also be a punishment written down that will be faced. The situation will appear very clear to both individuals, and the male sub will know exactly what is at stake if he disobeys his femdom. Depending on what rules the male breaks, the femdom might even enjoy locking him up in a cage for temporary periods of time until she feels that he has truly learned his lesson.

While you don't have to get this kinky in your relationship, you might feel curious about this kind of rule-breaking and obedience. Feel free to explore these things with your partner. If you would like, you can watch pornography that depicts these roles in a more intense way. These scenes can give you ideas for what you might want for your own relationship. The femdom might even feel more empowered after seeing other females acting in a kinkier manner. This all comes down, again, to personal comfort and how far you are both willing to take things.

You are both human beings. Even despite any written rules in place, if the femdom sees that you are struggling beyond what is considered pleasurable, then she is likely going to alter what she is doing. She might even change the rules because of it. A big part of being involved in an FLR is letting go of that fear and putting trust in your femdom. She knows what is best for you, and she will know how to challenge you in ways that you could never challenge yourself on your own.

As the male sub, you need to fully trust in your femdom's instincts. Since she knows what she wants, what she wants from the relationship, and what she wants from you, then you do not have to worry about doing a lot of extra work. You simply have to be obedient, follow your written rules, and ensure that you are making her happy at all times. Her needs and satisfaction are your new life priorities, and you should find fulfilling them to be quite enjoyable. Most subs are shocked by how much fun they have when they relinquish the traditional control they were once given.

Depending on how open your femdom is to suggestions, you might be able to put in some requests to alter your rules. Beware because if your femdom is not in the mood to hear this, she might punish you. Work with her to see if you can alter any of the rules to better support your satisfaction and comfort. If your request to change them is purely based on your safety and comfort, she is going to be more likely to give in. If your request simply has to do with you receiving more pleasure, then she is probably just going to take it away from you by withholding or having your edge. Femdoms can be tricky to bargain with, but this can become a very fun aspect of an FLR relationship. Each risk you take directly involves your role in the relationship.

As a male sub, it is very unlikely that you are going to be given the opportunity to write your own rules. This is just not how the typical FLR dynamic works. Your femdom might offer you the chance to do so as a test, but if you know what is best for you, then you would deny this and allow her to make the rules. If she asks you to keep the rules with you at all times, then you need to figure out a way to accommodate this request. Keeping this piece of paper a secret from the public and people you interact with on a daily basis can become fun. It is a nice and secretive reminder of the lifestyle you lead at home.

If you can sense that your femdom is becoming bored with the relationship or growing tired of being in charge, don't bring this to her attention. She is going to let you know if she ever gets to the point where she has had enough. From there, you will either transition back into a more traditional relationship with typical roles, or your femdom will have to switch up the kind of play that you are having. Any relationship takes work from both parties, and if you are both willing to put in this work, then there is no reason why the relationship needs to fizzle out in the first place. If you do want to make any suggestions, thank your femdom first. Tell her how great she is doing, and then suggest something fun that you think you might be able to incorporate into the relationship.

# Chapter 4:

# How to Begin

Perhaps you are reading this guide on your own, gathering information about the FLR lifestyle in order to tell your partner that you'd like to give it a try. This can be a nerve-wracking experience, as can any change in a relationship dynamic. With the help of this section, you can focus on the main points of what it means to be involved in the FLR lifestyle in order to best inform your partner about it. From the proper terms to use to the roles that are often taken on, you should have a greater understanding of all of these things by now.

Remember, if your partner truly loves you and cares about you, they are going to be open-minded to anything you have to say. If they seem hesitant about the idea at first, remind them that it does not need to happen all at once. There are always levels to FLR relationships, and there is nothing wrong with staying at the first level for a long while until you both truly feel that the lifestyle is going to work for both of you. As much as you'd like your partner to be open to the idea, be open to their feelings. Listen to their questions and concerns.

## Enforcement

The easiest way to begin is by having a normal conversation about it. Talk about what it means to be involved in the FLR lifestyle, and mention to your partner that you'd like to try it.

The worst thing that will happen is they will say they have no interest in taking part in such a lifestyle. Before you let them shut you down, see if they are willing to listen about exactly what is involved in this type of relationship. As you know, many people understand it only based on what is depicted on television and in the porn industry.

After explaining what is involved in an FLR, you can ask your partner how they feel about this dynamic. Talk about it in terms of how it would fit directly into your current life. Mention the current downfalls of your relationship and showcase how becoming involved in an FLR might improve these things. Most traditional couples enter an FLR because their old relationship became too stale, boring, or void of excitement. An FLR is designed to always be exciting and unpredictable. When the power has been shifted, this brings a whole new dynamic into the couples' life together.

You can test the water first by having one conversation about the lifestyle. Your partner likely won't be able to commit to anything right away because no matter which role you will be taking on, it is likely going to be a big change. Allow them the time to think about it on their own and then get back to you with any feedback or questions they might have. Likely, they are going to come back to you with several questions about how this all works. Since you have been looking into the topic for a while, you should be able to answer all of these questions and ease any concerns your partner might have.

If you find that your partner is starting to open up to the idea, this is great! You can then further your discussion by talking directly about which roles you will each be filling in the relationship. The roles are one of the more significant differences in an FLR versus a traditional relationship. Most of the time, these roles need to be entirely reversed in order to act on an FLR lifestyle. This means that both partners have to be secure in themselves and have trust in their partners before this is going to work out.

Talk about sex! Sex is a big part of the FLR lifestyle, and there will be a lot of changes occurring in the bedroom. Your partner is likely going to want to know everything about what is going to change regarding sexual pleasure, so be candid about this. Discuss all of the different ways that an FLR can be enforced sexually, and let your partner give their input on what they think about all of this. Much like any other relationship, compromises will be made. There might be some things that your partner is totally on board with, while other things might be off-limits. This is why discussing boundaries in the very beginning is so important.

Discuss how you feel about your privacy as a couple. If you decide to enter an FLR, do you want to tell anyone else about it? Can best friends know, but family members should be kept in the dark? This is something that needs to be made clear at the beginning of your relationship transformation. If you find that one partner is talking openly about the relationship, then this is, in turn, exposing both partners. Privacy is just as important as consent, so make sure that you respect it if your partner is willing to give an FLR a try.

You can make this a temporary trial until you both get a feel for what being in an FLR is actually like. Most couples can't imagine it until they are in it. And, as mentioned, it can take up to a month for you both to fully relax into your roles. If you are holding back in any way, it is just going to feel like a big role-playing session. An FLR isn't role-playing; it is two separate roles that you are both willing to take on and commit to. They should be taken as seriously as the relationship itself.

Talk to each other often about which aspects you love and which you do not care for. Modifications can be made as you try this new lifestyle out. Remember, there is no template for what an FLR needs to look like. The only defining characteristic is that the female is in charge. You can do with that what you will, to any degree you both feel comfortable with. Once you have consent from your partner, your experimentation can become very fun and often sexy. This is a big change, so you might see certain sides of your partner and yourself that you have never seen before.

# Degrees

Do you want your relationship to be loose, strict, or somewhere in between? You must discuss the which degree you both prefer at the beginning. Assuming you are both consenting and on-board, you can then decide to which degree of intensity you'd like to take your FLR. As a recommendation to beginners, it is best to keep it loose or somewhere in between at first until you both get used to the new dynamic. If you jump straight into the strict and hardcore stuff, this can become too much in such a short period of time. Make sure that you have this discussion with your partner, and if you can't come to an agreement, then you must come to a compromise.

As your relationship evolves and your comfort levels grow, you can try to change the degree of intensity as you wish. Since nothing is set in stone, you don't need to worry about 'making mistakes.' There is no such thing as being bad at an FLR. As long as you are following the main basic principle, then you are doing just fine. Let the relationship evolve naturally. While you both might crave more intensity right away, you need to make sure that you are both ready to handle it.

Being in an FLR tends to bring out very demanding and enticing sides of each individual. This is why your sex appeal can seem as though it is through the roof to your partner. While it can be tempting to just jump right into a hardcore BDSM relationship, you need to make sure that you are both ready to handle it. Any couple who once functioned traditionally normally needs a bit of a transition into that lifestyle before just trying to apply it into their own lives.

This doesn't mean that a hardcore relationship isn't possible, though. You can work your way up to it with your partner. Being in an FLR also gives you a renewed sense of partnership. You both must work together to come up with agreements, boundaries, rules, and playtime activities. It is definitely an effective way to reconnect with your partner for the betterment of your relationship. In the beginning, both partners need to be speaking up about the dynamic. Of course, once you are all settled in, the femdom is going to take over.

Do you want to include physical contact in your FLR? This might seem like a trivial question for some, as sex is one of the main things that couples in an FLR enjoy, but it is not applicable for all couples. Remember, some couples might be content with simply becoming a part of the FLR dynamic when it comes to doing work around the house and running errands. There are plenty of ways that a femdom can dominate without dominating her man sexually. Don't feel ashamed if this is how you need to start your FLR, or if this is as far as you want to take it.

Assuming sex is going to be a part of your FLR relationship, discuss whether or not there will be any pain-inflicting for sexual pleasure. For most couples, this can be answered fairly quickly. You either are into pain, or you aren't. Not everyone operates as a masochist/sadist, so don't feel bad if the thought of pain is too much for you to handle in the bedroom. If you do want to give it a try, be safe with it. Make sure that you do enough research to know when your partner has truly had enough and when the pleasure is actually becoming too dangerous.

Are you going to experiment with bondage? There are several ways for the femdom to tie up her partner, and not all of them involve ropes. You can use zip-ties, silk scarves, handcuffs, bedsheets, handcuffs, and more. Bondage does not have to be intricate and complicated at first. It can be anything that the femdom feels is right. No matter what form of bondage she uses, the male should also feel right about the experience. He should be grateful for the opportunity.

No one is going to be judging you when you are in the privacy of your own bedroom. If you do not know how to tie up your submissive male properly, you will learn how. He might break free a few times, and this will provide you with further motivation to keep him bound. You can also consider gags. This will prevent him from talking and making any noise, but also keep in mind that he won't be able to please you with his lips and tongue while he is gagged. A trip to the sex shop together can be a great learning experience for what kind of bondage you might want to get into. There are so many different props and toys available for your use.

## Levels

The next step is figuring out what levels and roles you are each going to take on in the relationship. As mentioned earlier, there are four levels of dominance. As the femdom, she needs to decide which one suits her best. After she figures out her dominating style, then the male can settle into his given role.

The femdom is going to be the one who controls the basic levels and roles of the relationship. Once she has the man's consent, then she should already be acting in her role and taking charge of what is happening in the relationship.

If the man has any reason to protest, he should do so at the very beginning. For a submissive male, it is a lot smarter to make suggestions rather than demands. This will place you in a much more vulnerable state of being (which you should be working toward in an FLR), and it will show the femdom that you respect her. She is going to then take your request into consideration, but this does not mean that she has to modify the dynamic in the exact way that you are suggesting. She might decide that nothing about it needs to change at all.

# Experimentation

In most traditional relationships, it wouldn't be common to think about anything that you do as a couple as an 'experiment.' When you are deciding on an entirely new lifestyle, though, experimentation is more common. Plenty of couples need a small period of experimentation before they can fully decide to commit to the FLR lifestyle. Keep this in mind as you begin with your partner. You do not *have* to stay in this type of relationship if it isn't serving both of you. This is why it is essential that you both know what you want out of the relationship.

Before you begin, during your communication stage, talk about exactly what it is that you both hope you can get out of the relationship change. Discuss what you want personally and what you hope to achieve as a couple. Some couples wish to enhance their sex lives, while others just want something new and exciting that is different from the norm. No matter what your desires are, keep them in mind at all times. They are going to guide you by letting you know if an FLR is right for you.

Take your first step and implement a single change in your relationship. As mentioned, the first step that a lot of couples make begins in the bedroom. When you have a new power structure during sexual activity, you are really going to notice the evolution of what your relationship could be like if it were a full FLR. Try this out and see how it feels; this is an experiment. The worst thing that will happen is that you will both agree that the lifestyle isn't for you. Things can then go back to how they used to be, and you can stay with a more traditional relationship.

If one partner is into the FLR, but the other is not, you can make modifications. With experimentation, nothing is set in stone. Maybe you will enjoy only certain aspects of being female-led in the bedroom, but not all. This is okay, too! Only do what you personally enjoy and what you and your partner are both comfortable with. Through these small steps, you might gain the confidence to try more things in the future. The most important thing is to take the pressure off of your relationship as you are in the experimental phase. It can lead to unnecessary stress.

Sometimes, starting in the bedroom isn't going to be your first step. You might want to begin with chores and errands. This is typically a fairly easy transition, and many couples who try this generally seem to enjoy it right away. From the female's perspective, this is a great change in pace. The male might not be used to taking on these tasks, but he should quickly get used to the role. This can be an experiment too, though. Sometimes, even the slightest power shift can lead to fighting or bickering. If this happens, then you will know that some modifications need to be made.

You might get several steps into an FLR before you realize that it just isn't the right lifestyle for you. Through this process, you can have several learning experiences. Maybe you don't want to commit to an FLR as a couple, yet you might want to utilize more female-led activities in the bedroom. No matter what you do, by trying out something new, you are going to be learning and growing together as a couple. Alternative lifestyles can bring couples closer together and renew that passion they once felt in the very beginnings of their relationships.

If you know that you are going to begin this lifestyle as an experiment, set a few timelines for yourselves. Try something out for a week or a month, and then check-in with one another. Talk about what you like and dislike about the change. From there, you can decide if you want to keep this aspect of the FLR in your life or get rid of it altogether. Keep doing this until you find the perfect balance and level of the relationship that you both desire to be in. The best thing is—only the two of you get to decide this.

When you are making these decisions together, you are automatically becoming a more communicative partnership. By deciding what works best for both of you instead of only requesting the things that you desire, you are making the relationship even healthier. If you decide to stay with a traditional lifestyle, the experiments can still help improve it just by the process alone. You will learn how to better talk to your partner about things, especially those that you do not care for. It is often harder for most people to talk about these things than the ones that are blissful.

# Long-Lasting

You might be wondering, can this type of relationship really last forever? Because of the stigma that has been built around alternative lifestyles, many people see FLRs, and relationships like it, only as fetishes. While it might be some sort of a fetish for you, that has nothing to do with the longevity of the relationship itself. Keeping the relationship going is solely up to yourself and your partner. It is no different than if you were participating in a traditional relationship. As long as you are both putting effort into it each day, then you have a high chance of succeeding.

The following are some tips to help ensure that you are both in it for the long run:

- Don't act: An FLR isn't equivalent to role-playing, so remember this. It isn't a game or some sort of play that you are acting in—this is your life. When you are both genuine about your roles and the level of dominance, then you have a much better chance of making the relationship last.

- Do it for yourselves: The only reason you should enter an FLR is that you both want to. There is nothing more complex about it. If you feel pressure from other people, pornography, society, or anything else to change your lifestyle, then it likely isn't going to serve its best purpose. The point is that you should both want it, and that is why you are making an effort to make it happen.

- Be honest: You might be in an FLR for ten years before realizing that it no longer makes you happy. While you gave it your all and wanted it to last, if something feels wrong, then you need to speak up. There might be ways that you can change the relationship while still keeping up with the female-led dynamic. Change can happen at any point in a relationship, new or old. Don't think that just because things have been the same way for so long that they cannot be altered.

- Have fun: Try not to take things so seriously. While a relationship is very important and relevant, it needs to be fun. It should be one of the things in your life that makes all of the stress and pressure dissipate. If you find that you are no longer having fun with your partner, then you can likely tell that something needs to change. While an FLR is known primarily for being a more fun relationship, it can still become stale if not enough effort is put into it each day.

- Be yourself: Don't lose track of who you truly are as a person while you are in the midst of your FLR. Though your roles in the relationship are changing, you are still the same individuals. Allow your personality to come through. If you try to put yourself into a category of how you expect the typical FLR couple to look, then you are actually going to be making it harder to achieve a long-lasting relationship.

A lot of couples wonder if they can genuinely incorporate the FLR lifestyle into every aspect of their lives. How are you supposed to act at the company Christmas party? Will dinners with family become weird? How will you describe your relationship to your best friend if she asks you how things are going? There tends to be a lot of pressure and unanswered questions that you might have about social settings and other normal things that you experience in your daily lives. As an FLR couple, remember that nothing needs to change externally. You don't have to display your main level of dominance outside of the home unless you both feel comfortable with it. You can tone it down a notch if you are in public or around loved ones who don't know about your lifestyle.

There are many ways that you can alter your FLR in order to fit the lives that you currently live. You won't know exactly how it feels until you give it a try. Some people are pleasantly surprised at how easy it is to modify the relationship to fit each appropriate situation. Others find it hard to keep the relationship balanced, and they often feel as though they are living double lives. This thought can be sexy, but it can also be complex. You both need to honestly gauge the relationship in all aspects of your life to see if it is going to work out. Remember that you can do as many revisions as it takes until you have the perfect level of dominance, the perfect roles, and the perfect display (or secrecy) about your relationship. The perfect balance is achievable, as long as you are both willing to work toward it in the long run.

# Chapter 5:

# Finding Balance

Once committed to your FLR, you are going to need to work on finding balance each day. Much like any relationship, there needs to be a healthy balance between romance, work, social life, self-care, and everything in between. This section will guide you through the process of finding this balance because an FLR can be more demanding than a traditional relationship. Since certain roles and rules are meant to be upheld, it can be a challenge for couples to maintain their lives and their newfound lifestyle. It isn't impossible, though!

Even the busiest people will have time for the things that they value most. Time is made when necessary. You can have a blossoming career, growing family, and other responsibilities while still maintaining a healthy relationship. For any FLR couple, there are bound to be periods where challenges will come up. This is normal. What matters most is that you are both able to work through them and realize that they are only temporary.

As an FLR couple, you need to prioritize your relationship even more than you would a traditional relationship. There is a lot of learning to be done, and that learning doesn't stop. You are constantly going to be learning new things about your dynamic and about yourselves individually. If you can make time to learn and listen each day, then you are going to be able to find the right balance to fit your needs. Life can be demanding as it is, so being in a demanding relationship can often be a test (especially for the male sub). Enjoy this, and think of it as a personal challenge to do better each day.

# How to Find Balance

There is no easy answer to the question of how to find balance in your life. It is something that must be thoroughly explored and discovered individually. As a couple, finding balance can be one of the most difficult aspects of any relationship. If one partner loses their patience, the other partner might end up feeling discouraged. It is important that you do not take these feelings out on one another, but instead, work through them together. Even if it isn't easy, it is worth it. Being happy with your partner, the person you wish to spend your life with, should always be worth it. Surely, in an FLR, there will be some sacrifices made. You will learn that this doesn't have to be a negative thing, though.

If you need to put some additional thought into it, you can make a pros and cons list. It might seem trivial, but it can truly help you decide if your FLR is a worthy addition to your current lifestyle. Weigh out the good parts and the bad parts of this type of relationship. Carefully consider each one. After you each make your individual lists, you can compare the two. This will give you both the chance to be honest and candid about the way that you each feel regarding the balance and the incorporation of the relationship into your life.

The list doesn't have to be the final word regarding your FLR. It can simply serve as another way for the two of you to really gauge if it is going to be the type of lifestyle that you can handle while not neglecting the other important parts of your lives. Having this list will also show each of you what the other values most. You can see if you are on the same page in terms of what you believe are positive elements and what you believe are challenging elements. This is a great exercise to complete as a couple no matter what type of relationship you are in.

Consider your future. Might there be anything happening in your future that you have planned that would interfere with your new relationship dynamic? While you can't always predict the future, there are some things that you might already know to be true. Consider these things as you decide if an FLR is going to provide you with a balanced lifestyle. If you have children, are they going to grow up seeing this aspect of your relationship? Do you want to keep it private? These are some real issues that a lot of FLR couples struggle with.

While, of course, you will be appropriate in front of your children, there comes the point where they might become old enough to catch on to the fact that daddy does everything, and mommy is the boss. This bothers some people, as it falls back on the same pressures that society places on humans every single day. The male is supposed to be seen as the head of the household. Many couples don't want their children to be teased or bullied because of a reversal of this power dynamic. This is a common thought that FLR couples consider, even if they do not have children yet.

Of course, there are ways to still have a 'normal' family dynamic while keeping the relationship dynamic female-led. You just need to work on finding this balance. Sometimes, this can only come through practice. There are certain things that you must experience first-hand in order to know how to handle them. Don't let them stress you out or discourage you from trying new things. Remember, this is no deadline or timeline as to when you need to fully transform your lifestyle. This is a very personal decision to be made as a couple, and you can take as much or as little time as you need.

Being a dominant female in public does not have to involve any extra attention from onlookers around you. There are subtle ways for the female partner to be dominant without anyone else even taking a second glance. Before even leaving the house, she can instruct her male partner to act a certain way or to do certain things. With him knowing what is expected of him before the couple is even in public, this is still a practice of public female dominance. Start out by trying to give your partner a few small rules or instructions to follow, and then you can work up from there.

As you both get used to this, the female can become even more vocal while you are around other people. Much like everything else about getting into an FLR, this part can be taken in steps as well. It can be a fun journey to take with one another, the male not knowing what is going to be expected of him until instructed. This gives the female a chance to control not only the power, but also the level of exhibition that is going to be displayed. There might be certain days where you will both feel extremely confident about your lifestyle and decide to be extra open about your actions. Give it a try, and definitely incorporate this into your experimental phase.

It might surprise you that you and your partner will become exhibitionists in the process. Glances from onlookers can turn into exciting nuances to look for while you are outside of your house. This is something that a lot of FLR couples feel is exciting and fun. The best part is—there is nothing wrong with it! A little bit of public foreplay can definitely replenish the passion in a relationship, making the activities that are done behind closed doors even more intense. There is no way to know for sure how you will both feel until you try it, but know that it could be worth a try. Do whatever it is that makes you comfortable and that the female decides is appropriate for the relationship.

Something that makes any type of relationship special is the secrets that are kept between the two people involved. By simply knowing what type of lifestyle you live and knowing that other people are curious, this can lead to some adrenaline rushes. This is the type of excitement that will allow your FLR to grow, and it will allow both of you to become more comfortable as you truly settle into your roles. Taking these steps will make your roles a way of life instead of a role-playing scenario. When you can accept that your FLR is your life rather than an external aspect of your life, then it will become easier to let go and be comfortable with this shift in dominance.

Think about the levels that you can take your public dominance. It can start with the femdom telling her partner how he must act and what he must wear, but it can evolve even further. As mentioned, there are also ways that she can sexually tease him in public without anyone knowing exactly what is going on. From wearing sex toys that are meant to keep him on the edge to forcing him not to touch her or look at her as she wears a revealing outfit, there are plenty of ways that an FLR couple can explore their levels of public dominance.

For the couples who are extra curious, try getting involved in an FLR community. With a little bit of research, you can find other FLR couples in your local area to connect with and form friendships. Sometimes, it helps to see other couples in action who are comfortable in their roles; it can be inspirational as a beginner couple. There is also the option of attending kink or fetish conventions together. During these events, FLR couples are often very public about their relationship because it is a safe place for this type of expression. You might see a femdom walking her male partner on a leash, or a man worshiping his femdom at her feet.

Being around other couples who practice the same kind of lifestyle can make a very big impact on your own relationship.

By seeing how free and open some of the other FLR couples in your area are, you will gain a sense of solidarity. It does help to know that you aren't alone in this and that others do enjoy the same kinds of activities. You will also probably find that there are always going to be couples that are more extreme in their practices. Again, without comparing yourself to anyone else, you can use these experiences and interactions to figure out where you'd like to take your own relationship.

## Everyday Routines

Everybody has a different set of routines that they follow every single day. Think about what you do as soon as you get up. You likely also have a routine before you have to leave your house and when you come home from work. What do you like to do on the weekends or in your free time? These routines are important to consider because if you can shift each of your routines a little bit, you will be able to make adjustments in order to shift your relationship from a traditional one to an FLR. It can sound like a lot of work, but think about it as something that is going to be beneficial and fun for both of you.

Starting from the very first routine, the femdom should control what happens in the morning. She is likely going to claim the bathroom to herself in order to get ready and comfortable first, as her routine is going to take priority over her sub's. Alternatively, she might like for him to get ready beside her, instructing him how she would like him to dress today and requesting any changes in his appearance that she might want him to make. Of course, this is going to vary depending on what your regular morning routine is currently.

The femdom can request for her sub to prepare breakfast and coffee each morning, serving it to her before they both leave the house. Since he is already going to be responsible for the household chores and duties, this should be something that he feels grateful to accomplish. She can also have her sub organize her belongings and get her bag packed full of all the things that she will need throughout her day. This is usually going to be the point where the femdom will make her sub wear a ball clamp or some other type of chastity belt if she wishes to keep him on edge all day.

Communication throughout the day is, of course, up to the femdom. She might not want to hear from her sub until they both rejoin at home later on in the day. There are other times where she will expect her sub to check-in regularly and keep her updated on how his day is going. Have fun with this communication when you are not together. Your texting or calling can get very heated, building up to what is to come later on in the night. Make sure that the femdom is being clear about how frequently she wants to communicate with her femdom while they are not together. This should probably be written into the set of rules that she creates.

After work, the femdom might want to go out and have some time to herself. Whether she goes shopping with a friend or goes out for some drinks, the sub is not to question anything about her actions. She will typically want her sub to stay at home, preparing dinner or doing other household chores and waiting for her to come back home. If the male sub would like to do something after work, he should have to ask him femdom for permission first. Depending on her mood and his behavior, she will decide if he has earned this privilege or not. This gives the sub even more incentive to behave properly and to act as the femdom wishes.

When you rejoin as a couple, the femdom is likely going to check-in with the sub to ensure that he has acted accordingly. If there were any miscommunications or mistakes made, then punishments might come next. Assuming that the femdom is pleased with the way that the day has gone so far, she will then decide what the couple will do to unwind. It might be something as simple as spending some quality time together in front of the television or practicing some bondage and other BDSM. Because the femdom gets to decide, the male is never going to know what to expect. His needs are secondary, and he enjoys pleasing his woman.

Having sex every single day isn't a realistic expectation. If you didn't have sex every day as a traditional couple, then this probably won't change drastically when you enter an FLR relationship. This is a common misconception that is made about couples who partake in alternative lifestyles. The femdom isn't always going to want to have sex, but there might be times when the sexual activity is going to be more frequent. It is going to fluctuate just as much as it would with any other relationship. You will both find the right level of sexual activity that it takes to please the femdom as you explore your new lifestyle. In the beginning, it might be heightened because it feels new and exciting again.

When you first started dating your partner, you likely had a lot more sex than you are currently having. This is normal for all couples in all relationships. Once you become more comfortable with one another, you tend to move out of this hyper-sexual phase and into one that is more settled and content. It can be incredibly hard to find the balance between holding onto this passion yet being your completely true and open self in front of your partner. You will know one another's flaws, yet there should still be many attractive qualities that you can admire in one another.

A lot of women in traditional relationships begin to feel less sexy and less desired as time goes on. Men also tend to get lazy, paying less attention to the woman's needs. In an FLR, the woman's needs are no longer going to be overlooked. If your femdom wants an orgasm, then you need to give her one. It is a true shift in power, and this is why it can seem that your level of sexual activity will pick up again. Know that if it lessens, this is also normal. Your femdom is going to decide how much sex you will be having, and as a submissive male, you must ensure that you are thankful for every single time that you get to have sex with her.

While you might not literally be required to worship your femdom, you do need to express your gratitude toward her when she allows you to have pleasure. Any time that you get to touch her or look at her, you should also express your thanks. This is likely going to please her very much and make her feel valued; this is the main element that tends to be missing in traditional relationships. When a woman is valued, she will feel confident. This is how your femdom is going to become as powerful as possible and reach her full potential as a dominant woman. This process can be exciting to watch for the male sub. The transformation will create a new spark in the relationship that likely existed in the very beginning.

Your daily routines don't always involve sex, but they do involve communication and basic instructions. As long as the femdom is happy at the end of the day, then the routine is working well for your FLR relationship. As a sub, it is important to make sure that you are keeping her happy. Even if she does not instruct you to do anything differently, yet you notice that she is unhappy, you should do everything that you can to behave in a way that will please her. No different than a traditional relationship, FLR couples will also go through phases where they will realize that they need more communication.

You might not have to change very much of your daily routine in order to transform your relationship, but you do need to be open to the idea that change is going to come. Both of you should expect at least some levels of change in order to properly fulfill your roles and keep your femdom happy. Being in an FLR does not have to be hard or a struggle. It can actually be very easy if you are both aware of the femdom's needs and willing to put in the effort to fulfill them.

## Tips to Make Both of You Happy

Demand alone time: When a femdom wants to do something alone, she should be able to do so without question. Whether she wants her man to stay at home or will allow him to go out and do something as well is up to her discretion. As the male sub, getting enough alone time is important; everyone needs some alone time every once in a while. If you are the male counterpart in the relationship, you must make it a point to earn your alone time. Show your femdom that you deserve to be able to have some small freedoms every once in a while. This will keep the FLR as balanced as it can be without stressing either partner out.

Respect personal time: As a male, if your femdom does not allow you to have alone time when she is having alone time, respect this. You need to let go of any remaining control that you are holding onto and simply let her live her life as she wishes. Do not check-in with her or question her as to when she will be back or what she is doing. This is how you can prove to your femdom that you are being a respectable sub. Taking this step back can be difficult for men who have been conditioned to take on a more dominant role, but it is possible to rewire your brain in order to curb this behavior.

Understand your growth: Sometimes, punishments aren't going to be fun for the male sub. They can be humiliating and embarrassing, but they must be endured if the femdom decides that they are necessary. Remember that these moments help the FLR grow. They help to enforce the femdom's power while showcasing how obedient the male sub can behave. As a femdom, you might have some moments where you question your own actions. Believe in your gut instincts about your relationship. If you have desires and needs, know that they are valid. By acting on them, you are growing into a dominant female, and this is exactly what it takes in order to be a part of a successful FLR.

Thrive on exclusivity: Knowing that you both have an agreement to remain exclusive to one another can serve as a small reminder that what you share is special. Only you know your partner in this way, and the same can be said for the way that they know you. No matter what kind of relationship you are in, excluding those that are non-monogamous, exclusivity is one guaranteed way to remind you that the connection you share is special and private. No one else is going to get to create the rules that you have in place, and no one else is going to follow them or enforce them other than the two of you.

Implement changes: As discussed, you are likely going to be experimental during your first few weeks, or months, as an FLR couple. If you both feel that changes need to. be made, do not delay these changes. The sooner that you make them, the happier you will both feel. By coming together as a couple and making these decisions, you are working on strengthening your bond. Although, as the relationship evolves, the femdom is going to be the one to implement all of the changes. Regardless, if she feels that something needs to change in order to better the relationship, allow this to happen sooner than later.

Go the extra mile: This pertains mostly to the sub, but when you feel like doing something extra, go for it! If you know that you can do something that will surely please your femdom, show her how much you appreciate her. While there are certain times that it makes more sense to stick to the rules, you will know when you can deviate a little bit in order to display your devotion to her. As a sub, there is a fine line between obeying and using your gut instincts in order to guide you as to how you should be acting in the relationship. This might involve a test of the balance, but it can be worth it if you do something that truly pleases her.

Listen before speaking: Another tip that involves action taken by the sub male—listen to your femdom before you speak. If she has something to say, this should take priority over what you are going to say. Consider her words carefully because she might be testing you. The way that you show her your obedience is going to directly impact how many rewards you get. In general, it is a good idea to listen to your partner before you launch into your own narrative. It shows that you are considerate and willing to take their feelings into account before you talk about your own.

Don't compete: When a femdom instructs her sub to do something, there should be no competition or power struggle in place. This is not the same relationship structure that an FLR should follow. While there are other power-play relationships that you can be a part of, the point of being in an FLR is that the sub is supposed to listen to his femdom. There should be no aspect of competition or reluctance when given orders. If you do try to turn things in a competition, you are surely going to frustrate your femdom and she is probably going to turn to punishment or withholding.

Understand your emotions: In an FLR, you both might experience certain emotions that you have never felt before.

Try to understand them for yourself before you act on them. As the male sub, there might be a sense of timidness or shyness that was never present before; it can often be very unfamiliar. As the femdom, there is sure to be a stronger sense of power and potentially even aggression. Understand that these new feelings are normal because you are changing a very big aspect of your life. Try to navigate your way through them and see how they fit in as you take on your new roles.

Keep your partner in mind: Even when you are not with your partner, you should be thinking about them. This is a natural part about being in a relationship, and it becomes especially relevant if you are in an FLR. Both of you might start thinking about one another more often, contemplating what is to come from your relationship. Whether you have been away from one another for a few hours or a few days, being in an FLR can teach you the important lesson that distance can definitely make the heart grow fonder. As the male sub gets settled into his role, he will begin to crave the discipline that he receives from his femdom. On the other hand, the femdom should also crave the obedience that her sub gives her.

Be respectful: If there is one thing that your FLR will teach you, it is that the concept of respect will be magnified. Respect is a very big factor in having a successful FLR. The sub must always know his place and show his utmost respect for his femdom. This practice is what sets the relationship apart from a traditional relationship. When the femdom sees how much her sub respects her and follows her orders, this is going to make her incredibly happy; it is the foundation for this type of relationship.

Keep your promises: No matter who is making the promise, it should always be kept. This is true in any relationship. The act of making a promise to your partner is one that is considered very special and personal. When they follow through with what they said they were going to do, this makes you feel important. A lot of happiness stems from kept promises, and a lot of struggles can ensue from broken ones. Try not to make any promises that you cannot keep, especially if you are in the role of the sub. It is a simple yet important philosophy.

# Chapter 6:

# Men: How to Attract a

# Dominant Female

So far, this guide has provided you with plenty of information on how to transform a current relationship into an FLR. This chapter will focus on a single male's perspective. From understanding the desire for a female-led relationship to finding the right woman for your life, you will learn everything you need to know if you are starting from the very beginning. Finding a partner, in general, can be difficult because there are many factors that need to align. When you are searching for a woman who can fit the role of a femdom, a few more factors are added to that list. This is why it is important to be prepared as you seek out the right woman for the job.

Whether you have acted as a sub in the past or this is your first time in the role, there is going to be a woman out there who will be able to fulfill your needs. Once you build up your confidence, you will know everything that you need to know in order to attract the right woman in your life. It takes patience, and you might have to enter more than one relationship before you find 'the one.' As long as you are aware of this before you seek out a romantic partner, then you should have no problem in waiting for the right one. Not every woman is going to be suited for the femdom lifestyle, even if she seems dominant in her everyday life. You must keep this in mind in order to remain hopeful.

You would be surprised that even the meekest woman might turn out to be the perfect fit for a femdom role. This is why you must truly get to know a woman before deciding if she can or cannot fulfill your needs; don't judge a book solely by its cover. Finding the right partner is a process, and the more effort that you put into it, the better results you will see. Try to secure your confidence in your role before you seek out your partner, and you will be sure to attract the right kind of energy into your life. By being your true self, you are showing all of the women you encounter what they can expect from being in a relationship with you. This takes courage, and in the end, you will be glad that you had this courage.

## The Desire for an FLR

If you are a single man who is thinking about entering an FLR relationship, you might be wondering why you are leaning toward this type of dynamic. Those who are unfamiliar with the lifestyle can often find different taboo reasons as to why a man might feel this way but know that there is nothing wrong with the desire. You might be tired of society painting a picture of how you need to act in a relationship. Maybe you want to tap into your vulnerable side in a big way. Think about your own personal reason as to why you crave such a dynamic. Know that it is not a bad or wrong way to feel. They are your feelings, so it makes sense that you would stay true to them. Being able to do so takes a lot of courage and confidence that you will grow to learn.

Being in an FLR, you might receive the comfort that you crave. As a man, it is often seen as a weakness to want this type of comfort. For this reason, a lot of men seek out traditional relationships because they believe that they are not as deserving of this comfort as a woman is. You might also just genuinely want more excitement in your love life—this is perfectly valid, too. The more that you read about FLRs, the more you might realize that a traditional relationship just isn't going to give you everything that you need in terms of excitement and passion. There is a lot for a male to gain from an FLR that those in the traditional relationship setting sometimes do not understand.

In terms of the satisfaction that you will receive, this comes in both sexual and non-sexual ways. Remember, an FLR isn't all about the sex. While this can be a big component of any alternative relationship style, know that it isn't the only one. Much like any other relationship, there are several different factors about being involved with someone that can bring you pleasure. You might feel lucky just to belong to such an amazing femdom, no matter what you do behind closed doors. Being able to fulfill a role and be rewarded for it can also bring you great satisfaction. It is like being good at your job and being acknowledged for it.

Is there a type when it comes to the kind of male that craves this lifestyle? There isn't a simple answer to the question. Looking at the obvious traits though, it can be said that the typical male sub who is seeking a femdom wants relief from his current expectations. This man likely wants to feel okay with being submissive without any judgment from the public eye or even from the woman that he is involved with. There are a lot of stigmas that surround male vulnerability, so it is typical for a man who wants to break free from this that seeks out an FLR. Perhaps you are tired of being expected to hold your feelings back and put on a tough exterior and rightfully so, because you are only human. You deserve to express yourself.

You have likely heard the term 'mommy issues' before, and a lot of people would argue that a man who craves an FLR has them. This is yet another stigma that surrounds the lifestyle.

When people see that a male wants to be cared for by a female, they might come to the conclusion that he wasn't properly cared for as a boy. Many believe that men who were raised in households with the lack of a mother figure or an unstable mother figure will tend to seek out romantic partners later in life that can also fill this role. There is some truth to this statement, but it isn't as negative as most people make it sound. Craving a nurturing partner is not wrong. You deserve to be cared for, and if you can find a femdom who is willing to fill the role, then you should feel happy that you've found her.

Personality types of male subs can vary greatly. You might be a very introverted individual, or you might take on a more extroverted role in your daily life. Either personality can still crave an FLR dynamic. The personality that you have seems to have little correlation with the relationship that you want. Your desires can change throughout the years, but your personality is typically established from a very young age. This is why it is unfair to say that only shy men would seek out an FLR. Men of all calibers can seek out this type of relationship. It is important that you do not feed into the stereotypes that are put in place because this will only fuel them. Break free of the mold, and don't be afraid to set your own example of how a man 'should' act.

Men who hold different careers can have the desire to become a part of an FLR. From those who work average jobs to those who are on very successful and prominent career paths, the desire does not discriminate. The lesson repeats—just because you feel that you do not fit the profile of what a submissive male does for a living does not mean that you aren't suited for the lifestyle. How successful you are as a professional should not make any impact on your FLR. You might have to take on a very dominant role at work, but at home, this dynamic can be entirely different. This is what makes the concept of an FLR so exciting. It gives all men the chance to experience this role reversal in a fun way.

You should be more familiar, now, with the idea that there isn't only one type of man who can become a great sub for a femdom. No matter what you do or have done before, your need for this type of relationship dynamic is valid. You deserve to find a partner who can give you what you want and who will receive all that you have to give. The alternative relationship community can be very private, but once you realize that there are local women who want the same thing that you do, it can provide you with a nice sense of solidarity.

Much like you would if you were already in a relationship, you can do some research on local communities in your area. Doing this online will probably give you the best results. Take a look at some websites that are geared toward the FLR lifestyle and try to find people nearby who are part of the community. These people can guide you in the right direction, and you might even develop connections through meeting them. This part takes a lot of courage. Once you get past the point of accepting yourself, you must be willing to put yourself out there in order to grow. Remember that this is a necessary part of getting what you want out of your love life. Everyone who is in a successful FLR also had to experience this part that you are on right now, so there are others out there who will be understanding.

The idea that no one has it all figured out from the beginning should be enough to put you at ease and encourage you to move forward in your pursuit of an FLR of your own. While there is endless research that you can do and so many people that you can talk with about the topic, the next step begins when you can actually get out and meet women who you feel that you would want to enter an FLR with. As stated, this can be a process of trial and error. It is going to be a learning experience, so remember to have fun while you are doing it. Not all of your dates are going to be amazing, but once you find the right connection, you will know it. If a spark exists, it should exist organically.

## Factors to Consider

While there is plenty for you to consider in terms of the kind of woman you'd like to date, you must also consider your current lifestyle. Do your current habits and routines align with those of an FLR? For most men, changes must be made in order to truly commit to an FLR lifestyle. This is normal, as it is for couples who are also entering the alternative relationship community for the first time. For this reason, you must be flexible. You need to keep in mind that you might need to change things that you have been doing for years, perhaps your whole adult life, in order to make an FLR a reality. If you are inflexible with your routine, then you cannot expect to successfully maintain any type of relationship.

Do you live alone, or do you live with others? This is a big factor that must be considered when entering an FLR. Because you are going to need a certain degree of privacy, you need to gauge your comfort level when it comes to inviting women to your home and having them spend the night. This isn't as much of a big deal if you live alone, but if you live with others, know that you are going to have to be comfortable with them seeing the way you interact with your femdom. In the beginning, it is likely that your level of comfort when it comes to being submissive in public is going to be very minimal. The people you live with likely won't even notice the dynamic if you don't want them to. Just keep in mind that you should consider this when you are beginning to date a woman who might be the right femdom for you. Of course, the two of you are also going to privately discuss your own levels of comfort in terms of what roles will be taken and to what degree.

Can you separate work from play? Some men might have to make a big switch when they are at work versus when they are at home with their femdom. Those who tend to work dominant roles typically enjoy being able to come home and undo this expectation. It can be a lot to get used to in the beginning, though. If you are someone who is expected to take the upper hand at work, think about your role at home as a release of all the expectations that you are holding onto in the professional setting. Know that you can let them all go and explore different parts of yourself when you are alone with your femdom.

Maybe your job already puts you into a submissive position. In this case, you can think about your time at home as a way of getting deeper into this submissive mindset. If you do not work a job that requires you to be a supervisor or other figure of authority, it can be fairly easy for you to slip deeper into this role in your love life. Use this to your advantage and allow yourself to become even more submissive. Men who are willing to do this are usually able to make their FLR a success. Remember, FLRs do not discriminate. Even if you work a job that is anywhere in between the two roles, you must still find your own personal balance for how you need to act at work and how you will need to act with your partner.

Family life is something that a lot of men will also consider. Whether you have kids or want them in the future, this is another big factor that needs to be taken into account when you are going to seek out an FLR. You need to make sure that your femdom is on the same page with you in not only wanting to start a family but also parenting styles that will be used. This is no different from any other relationship, but it should be stressed so that it is not forgotten when seeking out an FLR. It sounds like a simple concept, but it can easily be overshadowed by other factors when you are first entering the alternative relationship community.

Another aspect of family life that men must consider is how open they plan on being about their relationship with their family members. Even if you do not live with your relatives, you will want to consider how, or if, you will want to introduce the idea of an FLR to your immediate relatives. You can have a successful FLR without mentioning the concept to your family at all. Even if they were to meet your new partner, her dominance does not have to be at the forefront. You might feel very comfortable with the idea of your new lifestyle, and you might decide that you want to share it with your family. This is okay, too. Listen to your instincts and do what feels most comfortable to you. Remember, this can change as your relationship evolves.

There is likely someone in your life who you'd like to talk to about your FLR and your desire to find a femdom. This might be a close friend or just someone who you feel might be open-minded to the idea. It is a great thing to have a support system in your life, even if it only consists of one person. Being able to talk openly about your future relationship to someone that isn't your partner is a healthy practice. Plus, this is going to be something that is brand new for you. You'll likely have a lot to say about the experiences, so tell your friends that you trust. It can be a nerve-wracking step, but those who truly care about your happiness will support you no matter what.

The final factor to consider is your comfort level regarding being in public with your femdom. If you are dating femdom women who are experienced, they are likely going to take charge right away, and this could potentially include public social settings. Make sure to mention if you are or are not comfortable with this possibility before you go out on a date. It can often be exhilarating to simply immerse yourself in the lifestyle, as long as you feel secure in doing so. Your femdom can guide you toward a direction that you might truly want, but you might need a little push to get there.

If it makes the process easier, try to go on a date outside of your hometown. This makes it less likely to run into someone that you know, and you will feel more comfortable being your true submissive self in public. Plus, being in an atmosphere that is not familiar to either one of you sets an even playing field. You will both be able to naturally settle into the roles that feel right given the dynamic that is shared. Don't be afraid to speak up about what you want out of the relationship. If you desire punishments and bondage, talk about these things. Your femdom will likely have plenty of ideas in store for you by the time the date is over.

While there are plenty of factors that you should consider, keep an open mind the entire time. If you focus too much on these factors and not enough on what you truly desire in your heart, you might be limiting yourself. You are your own toughest critic, so give yourself a break! Know that you are a desirable submissive man and that there is a woman out there (or many women) who can provide you with the dominance that you crave. Explore freely and learn from any mistakes that you make. If you do not have a connection with someone, you cannot force it. This is something that happens naturally, and it is to no fault of your own or her own. Remember, if you click, then you'll know it. The right femdom should excite you, yet challenge you. She should be intimidating in the best way, but you should also feel comfortable with the idea of getting to know her on a deeper level. She is out there waiting for you, as long as you are willing to look.

# Finding the Right Woman

Everything has been considered, and you have been building yourself up, so what do you do next? Meeting women is challenging as it is, but meeting a woman who is willing to control you and give you all of the femdom qualities that you desire can be a whole new level of difficulty. Remember, you need to be patient. Finding a true connection cannot be forced, so keep this in mind as you are dating around. It helps to find out about your local alternative relationship communities. If you can get involved in one online, this is likely going to be the easiest way to find what you are looking for. Women who are a part of this community are already going to know that you are seeking an alternative relationship dynamic, so that saves you the big task of having to explain it.

If you can, become involved in message boards or chat rooms. While this might not be your typical method of securing a relationship, it can be very successful when it comes to finding an FLR. Getting to know someone online before you meet in person has become a standard practice in today's dating world. Even for those who are looking for traditional relationships, online dating is no longer seen as something that is bizarre or unnecessary. Nearly everyone has some sort of online presence, so it makes sense to explore with a woman this way before you decide if you'd like to take it to the next level.

When you are talking to a femdom online, maintain your role right away. She is likely going to guide the conversation, but you should also know that you can show her where you stand. Be submissive and open to her directions. This can be a fun and safe way to explore this side of yourself, one that you might never have explored before. If you do find that you are connecting with someone, she is likely going to propose the idea of meeting up in person. It is a good idea to leave this up to the femdom because it follows the relationship structure of an FLR. The female is going to take charge and do what she feels is right. This is how you will know if she is feeling the connection too.

Understandably, it isn't always possible to find a strong FLR community in your area. Sometimes, it might seem entirely impossible. If you cannot seem to find any resources that allow you to connect with people, you can try other forms of online dating. There are many dating apps and websites that are actually designed for kinky, or alternative, relationship arrangements. Whether you opt for one of these, or for something more basic like eHarmony or Tinder, these are all valid ways to meet women locally.

Make it known that you are looking for an FLR from the very beginning. It is going to be a waste of time if you connect with someone before bringing up this topic because they might not feel the same way that you do. You need to know that the woman you are talking to is on the same page from the beginning. As you know, not all people are suited for the FLR lifestyle. Whether you are on an alternative dating website or a traditional dating app, try to bring up the idea of being in an FLR as soon as possible. You will be able to get a candid response while also making it very clear as to what your expectations are. If you find that you do not align in this way, you can end the conversation and spare any hurt feelings.

Being upfront when you are dating is always going to lead you to the best results. If you are clear about what you want, this leaves little room for miscommunication and confusion once you begin getting involved with a woman. There will be nothing to stop you from believing that she desires you in the way that you truly want her to desire you. Honesty will get you a lot further in your dating life than holding back. If you hold back any part of yourself, it could come as an unwanted surprise when you finally do gain enough courage to mention it. This is why it is important to build yourself up *before* you begin talking to women. You will need this confidence from the very first conversation that you have.

Of course, you do have the option of meeting someone in person and testing the boundaries in a more traditional way. Perhaps you go out and meet a woman that you truly connect with, then how can you take it further? The honesty policy still applies. Once you get to know each other, explain to her what you are looking for. Since you will be in front of one another, it should be fairly easy to see if she is into the idea or not. She might be a first-timer, as well. When you are both on the same level, it can be a nice experience to grow together. Alternatively, if she has been dominant before, it can also be great because she will already know how to lead the way.

Only you have any way of knowing who the right woman is for you. As long as you are both consenting adults, it is up to you to gauge the chemistry that you share. You might both be on the same page regarding an FLR, yet the connection still won't feel right. This is natural, and it can happen simply due to two incompatible personality types. Make sure that you are sensitive to this feeling and do your best to always acknowledge it. If it goes ignored, you might end up in a relationship that is not as fulfilling as you hoped it would be. If you have ever dated at all in the past, you should have an idea of what it feels like when you can connect with someone on a level deep enough to take it to the next stage.

If you do need some friendly advice, talk to your support system! You don't necessarily have to disclose all of the details about the FLR aspect that you are looking for, but it can be nice to have someone to talk to about these new women that you will be meeting. It might even be a good idea to get together in a public setting with your friends and her friends at the same time. Mingling while others are around can add an extra rush of adrenaline to the situation. See how discreet she can be, or how open she chooses to be. This will be an exciting experience for someone who has never been involved in an FLR before. Still, it all comes down to consent. The boundaries that you set in the very beginning are the ones that need to be kept. Even though she is the femdom, she should still be respectful of your wishes. If she ever crosses any of your hard lines, then you need to have a serious discussion about it.

At the end of the day, no matter how you meet her or how long you two talk before you start dating, you are going to know if a woman is right for you. Try not to let society judge or influence you any more than it already has. You are an individual, and your needs are important. There is no need for you to feel that you have to fit into a certain standard mold because there isn't one. Anyone can be involved in an FLR, even those who don't appear to be into kinky relationships or sexual activities. You can never judge anyone's preferences just by looking at them, so it is important that you truly get to know someone before you rule them out entirely.

# Chapter 7:

# Sample Relationships

While you have read about all of the different components of what is involved in an FLR, it helps to read about real-life situations that involve these relationships. Hearing these stories might help you to decide if an FLR is right for you. All three of these relationships vary in the degree of how extreme the couple is with their actions. They will give you the chance to see that there are other people that you can potentially relate to. Sometimes, seeing things from this perspective can give you enough of a confidence boost to go out and live your life exactly as you want to.

Being able to read about FLRs in this context might make things clearer for you. Not only will you be able to see how you can experience this for yourself, but you will also get to see several examples of ways that these couples have achieved success with alternative relationships. It is possible, and though it might feel this way, you are not the first person to experience these struggles and these insecurities. You can overcome them. And whether you are a femdom or a submissive male, you will be able to find the person who is right for you and right for your life.

The following are three different stories of FLR couples who all met each other in different ways. In the ways that they choose to live their lives, they all bring forward some unique aspects to consider when seeking out your own FLR. Hopefully, by reading about these experiences, you will feel inspired and empowered. You will be able to see that there is a lot of diversity in the alternative relationship community. No one else is going to be going through exactly what you are going through, but you might find some commonalities in the experiences of others.

# Real-Life Relationships

## *Amanda and Carl*

The pair met when they were in high school, a typical story of juvenile love took place from the tender age of 15. Both Amanda and Carl were each other's first relationship; they experienced many firsts together. By the time that they were ready to start college, they were faced with their first major crossroads. Amanda wanted to stay close to home and attend a local community college for nursing, while Carl wanted to travel across the country to pursue his civil engineering program. Deciding that the distance was just too much, the pair made the painful decision to break up.

Amanda was able to move on quickly, focusing on her studies. Carl didn't know what to do without Amanda in his life; she took care of everything, and without her, he felt lost. This led to a lot of partying at his university, and it was during this phase that he experimented with other women. Sleeping with different women temporarily filled his void, but it did not fix any problems. Amanda thought about Carl frequently, but she never pursued any kind of romantic relationship or intimate relationship while she was in college.

It was six months before Carl was able to work up the courage to contact Amanda. He called her, explaining how he could not see his life continuing without her. She was taken aback, but receptive to his words. They began talking again, trying out a long-distance relationship. It was great in the beginning. As they reconnected and caught up on the things that they had missed in the last several months, they eventually ran out of ways to make the relationship feel fulfilling.

Carl made a big decision—he decided to leave his university and transfer to a school that was back in his hometown. He did this partly for Amanda and partly because he truly missed being back in his familiar surroundings. Once they were reconnected, sparks were flying. The relationship felt as though it were happening again from the very beginning. They went through a second honeymoon stage that left them infatuated with one another all over again. From this point forward, they decided that they never wanted to be without one another.

The next few years went by in a blur. As both Amanda and Carl graduated from college, they decided that it was time to take the next step. They got married and moved in together. It was a small apartment, but it was their own. The two of them fulfilled every aspect of the traditional relationship dynamic that was expected of them. Amanda soon became a mother to her first son. Her second son was born only two years later. After realizing that they needed more space, Amanda and Carl made their next investment—a house of their own.

They had it all; they were a big, happy family in a nice home. The two children were happy, and they all got along great. Because they were so close in age, they loved playing together and kept each other occupied. Amanda and Carl both worked fairly close to home, but the stress of being a nurse and a city planner was enough to make their nights full of complaints and empty of any kind of sexual desire. They eventually realized that they were living the lives that were expected of them, and they were getting bored. As much as the pair did not want to accept this fate, it was happening right before their eyes.

They tried couple's counseling, but it didn't feel right. Amanda thought it was stupid to let a stranger have this kind of insight into their love life. This only led to more fighting and bickering throughout the years. Carl was at a loss for what to do next. He was certain that he was about to lose his wife and his family. With a feeling of desperation, Carl asked Amanda about a big change regarding their love life. He had been reading about it online for quite some time, but he finally worked up the courage to mention it to his wife.

Amanda had no idea what an FLR was, and she was fairly reluctant to hear more. She thought that these kinky people were unlike her and her husband. Not into the idea of whips and chains, she was honest with Carl by giving him a candid reaction and looking at him as though he was crazy. Feeling discouraged, Carl tried to explain that there were different levels of this type of relationship. Amanda needed some time to take this all in. She wanted to make sure that she understood what her husband was asking of her. Never considered a dominant woman before in her life, she felt uncertain that she could play the role of a femdom.

It took an entire year for Amanda to finally open up to the idea. During an argument between the couple, Amanda decided to take charge. She had the mindset of a femdom at the moment, and it took Carl by surprise. The pair ended up making up and getting very turned on in the process, thus proving that the FLR lifestyle was actually going to work out for them after all. This began the true start of their alternative lifestyle. Because they had been together for so long, they knew one another very well. It took a lot for Carl to step down from his position of being the head of the household and allow Amanda to step up.

Clueless as to where to begin, the pair started in the bedroom. Amanda fully took over all of the sexual activities that the pair engaged in. She got to decide when they would have sex and when she would withhold pleasure from her husband. It became a very fun and exciting aspect of their relationship that truly revitalized their marriage. After becoming more comfortable with this change in power, they decided that they wanted to expand on their FLR. The household chores and other duties that involved errands were passed over to Carl. He willingly complied with these requests from his wife turned femdom, and pleasing her turned him on immensely.

When it came to what the children saw, the couple made a decision to keep the lifestyle something that was for their eyes only. The kids never saw mommy bossing daddy around, but they did notice a shift in the power of the household. Friends and family were kept in the dark about this change in lifestyle, but this only thrilled Amanda and Carl even more. They enjoyed the bond that they shared with each one, the one that only they knew about. It made the relationship exciting again, and it was enough to actually save their marriage.

Though they never decided to get into BDSM, the punishment was served in the form of humiliation and embarrassment. The couple never felt that being physically violent was a factor that fits into what they desired, but they did enjoy having a set of written rules posted in their bedroom for them to see at all times. Amanda and Carl didn't tell a single other person about what they did to help their relationship, but everyone took notice. They acknowledged that the pair seemed happier than ever. All they both knew to do was to look at each other and share a cheeky smile.

The FLR lifestyle worked for this long-term traditional couple when Amanda wasn't even sure if she could fill the role, to begin with. By giving it some ample time, she was able to think about it more clearly and realize that she did, in fact, have that dominant instinct inside; she had it all along. Only after she and Carl both consented to the relationship change were they able to make a difference in their marriage. They were both thankful that Carl decided to bring up this 'crazy' idea on that day because it became a true part of who they both were. Now, they are both thriving and ready to continue living their FLR well into their later years. They found a level that worked best for them and didn't give in to the pressures of what they read about online. Super happy in their roles currently, they both agree that they could never imagine going back to a traditional relationship.

## Sheila and Jason

Jason grew up with four brothers. He always felt different from them, but he could never understand why. With the same dark hair and an olive complexion, he was a good-looking young man. He was strong and popular in school, but he was never able to feel as charismatic as his siblings were. His only experience with romance came from short-lived flings that occurred throughout his high school years. He was never able to form true connections with the girls he dated because he felt that he was too soft. All of the girls that he talked to wanted a manly man. They wanted someone who would protect them, but in reality, Jason just wanted that for himself.

He continued his life with minimal experience in the romance department. After college, he finally met a woman who he felt that he could spend the rest of his life with. Karina was fun and interesting. She enjoyed being with Jason and seemed to accept him for all of his quirks. Unfortunately, their relationship began to unravel over the four years that they were together. Jason craved a caregiver, but so did Karina. When she brought up the idea of starting a family, this made Jason worried because he realized that he did not feel the same way. He didn't want to care for a wife and kids; he wanted a woman to care for him so that he could act like a kid. These thoughts confused him, and he tried to push them out of his mind.

Surely, this had to be wrong, he thought to himself. He felt like a pervert for even considering a lifestyle like this. He was also very hesitant to bring this up with Katrina, and his instincts served him right. After working up the courage to tell her how he felt, this truly worried Katrina. She felt wronged and betrayed; she thought that Jason had been leading her on for all this time. Through much explanation and pleading, he had to let her go because she was so rattled by the lifestyle that he proposed. He knew deep down that she was not the woman who he would spend the rest of his life with.

A lot of healing had to come after this, naturally. Jason isolated himself, and his childhood insecurities all seemed to return to him in full force. He didn't even want to leave his house, let alone approach a woman. He was scared that he would be rejected and that any other woman would also find his idea of living as an FLR couple crazy. After being alone for a very long time, he decided to break free of this pattern. Doing something very unlike his character, he decided to download a dating app. A person who was not apt on technology, to begin with, he didn't know what compelled him to do this.

The idea that there were so many women in his area that were single and looking made him regain hope in the idea that he could find what he was looking for. It took three months, but he finally connected with Sheila. She had a secret that she wanted to reveal to Jason, and it made him nervous. He thought that she was about to serve him some earth-shattering news, but she actually changed his life forever. She explained to him that she was only interested in a relationship if a man could handle her role as a femdom. Not knowing exactly what a femdom was, Jason was very intrigued.

They talked on the dating app for several weeks before finally deciding to arrange an in-person date. During this time, Jason was educated on the femdom lifestyle. He was taught that Sheila expects her man to wear certain clothing and act a certain way. She wanted to be addressed as 'Goddess,' and she needed to be in control of every single thing that happened in the bedroom. There would be no touching until she gave him permission to do so. She also made it very clear that her pleasure came first. Jason was very receptive to all of this, and the more he heard, the more this excited him.

Showing up in the suit he was instructed to wear, Jason sat down in front of his Goddess, nervously. She smiled and graciously placed her hand on his own for a kiss. He promptly complied. The night went on with this same energy, and Jason was so happy to know that someone who thought the same way that he did exist in his local area. As the night came to a close, Jason leaned in for a kiss. He was promptly slapped in the face before an entire restaurant. It stung, both physically and mentally. Sheila told him that she would love to see him again, but it was up to her to decide when they would share intimacy.

"I'm sorry, Goddess," he replied.

This seemed to please her, as she smiled and turned to leave. Admiring her frame, Jason was blown away by the best date he had ever been on in his life. He allowed Sheila to contact him first, waiting in anticipation. She agreed that it was time for another date. The pair continued their journey this way until Sheila finally invited Jason over to her place. She had a room that was unlike anything Jason had ever seen. Several whips, crops, and chains decorated her walls. The very first thing that she did was handcuff Jason to the headboard. This set the standard for the rest of their sex life.

After a few more weeks, Sheila agreed to take Jason on as her sub full-time. They came to an agreement that they were going to remain exclusive to one another, but Jason was to have no say in anything that pertained to the relationship. It was all up to Sheila, and they were both very happy with this arrangement. They were very public with their FLR, and one of the most public displays occurred on Jason's birthday. Sheila decided to take him out for a nice dinner, but during this time, he had to be leashed and collared. The pair definitely turned heads that night, but they were staying true to their desires. As the night came to a close, Jason was chained to his familiar post on the headboard and was given many different forms of teasing and foreplay before finally being given permission to get off.

While they had to face judgment from time-to-time, they didn't mind. They knew that the bond they shared was only their own, and they secretly enjoyed onlookers ogling them from afar. These instances in which they felt that they were on display fully brought out their exhibition tendencies, and they thrived on them. When they were finally alone at the end of each evening, they recounted all of the strange glances they received and laughed about all of the confusion that they were shown. Their story didn't start out in the most traditional way, but it started in the exact way that they needed it to.

As the pair became more comfortable in their relationship, they began doing more together. Jason was really able to receive all of the care that he craved so much throughout the first half of his life. Sheila had been doing this for quite some time, but she still found so much joy in the submissiveness that Jason was able to provide her. She thrived and became even more powerful in her ways. There were certain points where Jason felt scared, but he spoke up about each of them. Through these consensual boundaries, the couple was able to make their alternative relationship work. They learned how to do things that didn't cross boundaries, but instead, created excitement. This was the main element that allowed their relationship to become so successful.

## Paula and Will

The pair met after two individual failed marriages. Paula had given up on finding love because of her abusive past with romance. She wasn't looking for a man, or anyone, to fill that space in her life. It was only when she met Will by chance as both of them entered the same coffee shop one Monday morning that her mindset changed completely. Will's marriage ended on mutual terms—they had nothing in common. Though it was a painful end to eight years of dedication, Will was happy to be free to figure himself out again. In his marriage, he lost sight of who he was because he became so dedicated to his ex-wife's happiness that he forgot about his own.

Thinking that it would be a nice pay-it-forward gesture, Will decided to pay for Paula's coffee as he ordered his own. She stood in line behind him, beautifully dressed and striking. He had been admiring her since she walked in, but he didn't want to be too forward. After he received his Americano, he sat at a nearby table with no expectations. Paula was amazed that someone had thought to do this for her. Admittedly, she had been much more focused on her career since her marriage came to a close. A well-respected realtor in her local area, she felt taken aback that someone was kind enough to think of her.

She approached Will at his table and thanked him for the latte. After shrugging it off, he smiled and admitted that he had never done anything like that before. He just had the feeling that she could use a little bit of added kindness into her day, and he was right. Only hours before, Paula woke up to a check engine light in her vehicle in a day ahead that consisted of many miles of driving from property to property. Will, a writer, was settled down at his table for the remainder of daylight hours. He was working on his latest article for a local paper that he had a segment in.

Still not in the market for romance, Paula decided to take a chance and leave Will with her business card. She waved goodbye, and his breath caught in his chest. As he examined her card, he wondered if he would ever work up the courage to call her. A guy reserved in his daily life, he felt unsure about the way that women perceived him. As a self-proclaimed nerd and literature buff, it was hard to find women who understood his interests. He stored the card away for safekeeping, and it stayed safe for several months.

On his day off, after all those months, Will was tired of feeling lonely. He wanted someone he could connect with, someone to have a genuine conversation with. Dialing her number, he was doubtful that Paula would even remember him. She picked up after the second ring, always ready to answer her cell phone that doubled as her work phone. She was surprised to hear from him, and the conversation was indeed a little bit awkward. Will didn't know what to say, but he brought up the idea of a coffee date at the same spot where they originally met. Paula told him that she'd have to check her schedule and that she would call him back.

Thinking that he surely struck out, the pair hung up the phone. Will got up and stood in the mirror. A man of average height, he felt that he was below average in all other aspects of what was considered 'manly.' He had no facial hair, and he wasn't particularly strong. Secretly, he always felt like a disappointment to his previous partner because he felt that he couldn't be a protector. He just wanted love. These thoughts were soon interrupted by Paula calling him back. She agreed to meet him at the coffee shop in two days. Excited beyond belief, Will was already panicking over what he would wear and what he would say. She was way beyond his league, in his opinion.

The date was going very well. They actually had a lot in common, but Paula wanted to talk to him about something that she wasn't comfortable discussing in the public space of a coffee shop. She offered him a ride around town to view some of her current listings. These were neighborhoods that Will had never even been to before. He obliged, nervously opening the door to her pristine Lexus SUV.

"I am a femdom."

Will had never heard the term before, but he didn't want to strikeout. He asked her slowly and curiously about what that meant. He tried to place the word in his mind, but he had genuinely never heard it spoken before. The car ride consisted of beautiful views and a conversation that would change Will for life. As Paula explained her role, Will was growing increasingly horny. He felt ashamed for this, but it was the first time that anyone had excited him in a very long time. It was explained that Paula was dominant in every regard. She did not answer to any man, and in a relationship, she needed to be the decision-maker. Her expectations for any man that she dated had to be precise, or else consequences would be faced. Will pondered at the thought of these consequences, hiding the bulge growing in his pants.

As Paula dropped him back off at the coffee shop, she cheekily turned to face him. His face reddened as he realized that he probably looked very excited by the conversation. Smirking at him, she placed a single hand on his thigh. She knew exactly what she was doing, and she did it well.

"Do you think you can handle it?"

Will was even redder than before. He could only manage to nod his head. After she called him a 'good boy,' he almost got off right there in the passenger seat. Instructing him to kiss her, he obeyed gratefully. She forcefully pushed him back once she had enough, promising to see him again in a few days. This was the beginning of their unconventional love story.

They moved in together after seven months of dating. In the household, Will was made to do chores in a maid's uniform. He enjoyed every second of this, especially when Paula would enter the room in full latex attire and place a six-inch stiletto heel on his back as he scrubbed the floor. Sometimes, whips were involved. The pair became very kinky, and through this experience, Will realized that this is what he needed all along. Behind closed doors, anything could happen. What they truly loved to share as a couple was their secret of their FLR. When they went out in public, no one would cast a second glance at the seemingly-average pair.

Neither one of them told anyone else about the bond that they shared. While at home, Will was eventually made to wear a customized collar. The tag read 'Baby Boy.' Will loved belonging to Paula so much; he thrived on knowing that he was pleasing his femdom to the fullest extent. Sometimes, Paula would humiliate him, making him wear adult diapers and crawl around on the floor like a child. She laughed at him and took photographs that made their way into a private photo album.

The relationship continued to gain intensity as Paula introduced Will to many new elements of BDSM that he hadn't even fathomed before. A woman who was tired of men controlling her, she knew that becoming a femdom was the next step in her life. She wanted to keep Will forever, and he felt the exact same way. Punishments were intense, but the sex life that they shared was even more intense. Will could not imagine a relationship like this with anyone else, but he didn't want to. He became completely devoted to Paula and was willing to do anything for her. This excitement and dom/sub dynamic became the glue that held their intense relationship together.

# Conclusion

Female-led relationships can look different and can consist of different people with different personality types. Just because you have never done anything like this before or if you are unsure about the role that you are capable of handling, you will never find out unless you try it for yourself. Go slow at first if you need to. Make sure that you do plenty of research and try to reach out to others in the same community that is in your local area. Knowing that you are not alone in this desire, whether you are the femdom or the male sub, can make the experience a lot less daunting.

Just as personalities can differ, levels of dominance can also differ. Whether you want to explore hardcore BDSM practices or if you prefer a gentler approach, anything can qualify as an FLR as long as the femdom is in charge. Consider the femdom the leader of the entire relationship. She is going to put her needs first, and she will be providing instructions and rules that she decides on. As the male sub, you should feel grateful to have this guidance in your life. Being a sub greatly involves showing appreciation for your femdom at all times and enjoying making her happy.

There are always going to be different levels to take into consideration when you enter an FLR. You don't need to be a public display, yet you do not need to keep the fun completely behind closed doors either. You can do what is comfortable for both of you. With consent, anything is possible. Explore all of your wildest fantasies and make sure that you are both communicating with each other effectively. No matter what role you take on, it should align with your desires. You will know that you've found the right person when their desires also align with your own.

It is possible to find the right person to fulfill all of your needs; you must be willing to put in the effort to look for that person. It all starts with your basic level of self-confidence. Once you have mastered this, you will be unstoppable! In the way that you find others desirable, they will find you desirable because you know what you want out of your love life. There is no such thing as 'too much' when it comes to alternative relationships, and this is what makes them alternative. Don't be afraid to truly let loose and let others get to know the real you and what you truly want.

Thank you very much for considering this book your complete guide to FLR relationships. With this information, you can experiment and explore as much as you wish. Alternative lifestyles can be fun and exciting, but they can also change your life. Go forth, knowing that you have what it takes to express what you want and find someone who is willing to give it to you.

## The End

Thank you for buying my book and I hope you found it helpful and informative.

I would truly appreciate it if you left a review.

# References

FemDom: Why Every Woman Should Dominate Her Relationship |. (2014, September 5). Retrieved December 25, 2019, from https://conquerhim.com/femdom-why-every-woman-should-dominate-her-relationship/

Hasan, T., & Fauzi, M. (2012). If "women are from Venus and men are from Mars," does an answer lie with neuroanatomy?. International Journal of Collaborative Research on Internal Medicine & Public Health, 4(5), 566.

Hudson, P. (2014, February 13). 25 Ways To Have A Happy Relationship In Modern Times. Retrieved December 25, 2019, from https://www.elitedaily.com/dating/25-ways-make-relationship-last-modern-times

Power Exchange Levels. (2019). Retrieved December 25, 2019, from https://www.kinkly.com/definition/12056/power-exchange-levels

CPSIA information can be obtained
at www.ICGtesting.com
Printed in the USA
BVHW041245030521
606340BV00009B/2382